Also by Ross W. Greene, PhD

The Explosive Child:
A New Approach for Understanding and Parenting Easily
Frustrated, Chronically Inflexible Children

Lost at School: Why Our Kids with Behavioral Challenges
Are Falling Through the Cracks and How We Can Help Them

Lost and Found: Helping Behaviorally
Challenging Students (and While You're At It, All the Others)

RAISING HUMAN BEINGS

CREATING A COLLABORATIVE PARTNERSHIP WITH YOUR CHILD

Ross W. Greene, PhD

SCRIBNER

New York   London   Toronto   Sydney   New Delhi

Scribner
An Imprint of Simon & Schuster, Inc.
1230 Avenue of the Americas
New York, NY 10020

This publication contains the opinions and ideas of its author. It is intended to provide helpful and informative material on the subjects addressed in the publication. It is sold with the understanding that the author and publisher are not engaged in rendering medical, health, or any other kind of personal professional services in the book. The reader should consult his or her medical, health, or other competent professional before adopting any of the suggestions in this book or drawing inferences from it.

The author and publisher specifically disclaim all responsibility for any liability, loss, or risk, personal or otherwise, which is incurred as a consequence, directly or indirectly, of the use and application of any of the contents of this book.

Copyright © 2016 by Ross W. Greene

All rights reserved, including the right to reproduce this book or portions thereof in any form whatsoever. For information, address Scribner Subsidiary Rights Department, 1230 Avenue of the Americas, New York, NY 10020.

First Scribner trade paperback edition August 2017

SCRIBNER and design are registered trademarks of The Gale Group, Inc., used under license by Simon & Schuster, Inc., the publisher of this work.

For information about special discounts for bulk purchases, please contact Simon & Schuster Special Sales at 1-866-506-1949 or business@simonandschuster.com.

The Simon & Schuster Speakers Bureau can bring authors to your live event. For more information or to book an event, contact the Simon & Schuster Speakers Bureau at 1-866-248-3049 or visit our website at www.simonspeakers.com.

Interior design by Jill Putorti

Manufactured in the United States of America

20 19 18 17

Library of Congress Control Number: 2016021664

ISBN 978-1-4767-2374-7
ISBN 978-1-4767-2376-1 (pbk)
ISBN 978-1-4767-2377-8 (ebook)

For Talia and Jacob . . . the future is yours.

"Want to help someone? Shut up and listen!"

ERNESTO SIROLLI

You never really understand a person until
you consider things from his point of view . . . until you
climb inside his skin and walk around in it.

HARPER LEE, *To Kill a Mockingbird*

Grown men can learn from very little children,
for the hearts of little children are pure.
Therefore, the Great Spirit may show children
many things that older people miss.

BLACK ELK

Tell me and I forget.
Teach me and I remember. Involve me and I learn.

BENJAMIN FRANKLIN

CONTENTS

INTRODUCTION

Where We're Heading

Welcome to *Raising Human Beings*. I'm very glad you're reading this book. The mere fact that you're doing so suggests that you take parenting seriously and want to do it well. That's good; your kid needs you to think about what you're trying to achieve as a parent and to have the tools to accomplish the mission. If you've been feeling a little muddled about those things, that's understandable. These days, the guidance on how to raise kids is so ubiquitous and so incongruous that it's hard to know what's right and wrong, what's important and what's not, what to prioritize and what to let slide, and how best to respond when your kid isn't meeting expectations.

Let's begin by thinking about the most crucial task of your child's development: he needs to figure out who he is—his skills, preferences, beliefs, values, personality traits, goals, and direction—get comfortable with it, and then pursue and live a life that is congruent with it. As a parent, you have a similar task: you, too, need to figure out who your child is, get comfortable with it, and then help him live a life that is congruent with it. Of course, you also want to have influence. You want your kid to benefit from your experience, wisdom, and values and effectively handle the academic, social, and behavioral expectations of The Real World.

That balance—between having influence and helping your child live a life that is congruent with who he is—is hard to achieve. Most conflict between parents and kids occurs when that balance is out of whack. The collaborative, nonpunitive, nonadversarial approach to parenting described in this book will help you maintain the balance and keep the lines of communication open.

But, as suggested by the title, this book has a dual agenda. Yes, you definitely want things to go well in your relationship with your child, and you want your child to be able to handle the demands and expectations of The Real World. But you also want to parent in ways that foster qualities on the more positive side of human nature. We humans are capable of both altruistic and ignoble actions. Our instincts can lead us to acts of remarkable compassion and cooperation but also to lamentable insensitivity, conflict, and destruction. We have the capacity for characteristics such as empathy, honesty, collaboration, cooperation, appreciating how one's actions are affecting others, perspective taking, and resolving disagreements in ways that do not cause conflict. Those are characteristics that The Real World is going to demand. But they need to be cultivated and encouraged. The approach to parenting described in this book will help you accomplish that mission as well.

Like many parents, you may find it hard to maintain perspective on the kind of parent you want to be when you're caught up in the minutiae of everyday living. It's easy to lose sight of the big picture when every day you're consumed with your child's hygiene, homework, chores, sports, activities, appointments, friends, car pools, SATs, and college applications. But maintaining your perspective is worth the effort, not only for your relationship with him but because the challenges that face our species and our world are going to demand his and your best instincts and actions. We need to raise our game, starting with how we raise our kids.

Now, a brief word about me. I'm the father of two kids, both now in their teens, so I have some firsthand experience with the peaks and valleys of parenting. It's been the most fun and humbling experience of my life. I've also been a clinical psychologist for over twenty-five years, specializing in kids with social, emotional, and behavioral challenges. I've worked with thousands of kids in many different contexts: families, schools, inpatient psychiatry units, residential facilities, and prisons. Did my psychology training and experiences work to my advantage in parenting my own two kids? I suppose so. But just like everyone else, I had to get to know my children, figure out who they are, and take it from there. And I had to adjust at various points along the way, because those kids of mine kept growing and changing on me.

In my first book, *The Explosive Child*, I articulated an approach to parenting behaviorally challenging kids—the approach is now called Collaborative & Proactive Solutions (CPS)—that helps caregivers focus less on modifying kids' behavior and more on partnering with kids to solve the problems that are causing those behaviors. You'll be reading a lot about that approach in this book, because it's just as applicable to kids whose problems and behaviors are more typical. See, there's really not a whole lot of difference between "typical" kids and those who might be characterized as more challenging. Yes, some are more violent and volatile than others. Some are big talkers; others are quiet or completely nonverbal. Some come from fortunate circumstances; others have come down a much tougher path. Some live with their biological parents, others with one parent, or stepparents, or adoptive parents, or foster parents, or grandparents. Some have academic struggles; others have difficulty making friends; and still others struggle with overuse of substances or video games or social media. Some have lofty aspirations; others aren't thinking much at all about what the future holds.

But they all need the same thing: parents and other caregivers who know how to maintain the balance between expectations and the kid's skills, preferences, beliefs, values, personality traits, goals, and direction; who are able to bring that balance to everyday life; who help them participate in solving the problems that affect their lives; and who go about it in ways that foster the most desirable human instincts.

Because this book is relevant to children of both genders . . . and because it is cumbersome to read *he or she, him or her,* and *his or her* throughout the book . . . and because I didn't want to write the book in one gender . . . entire chapters are written in alternating genders. I've drawn upon a multitude of real kids and parents I've known and worked with in creating the characters in this book, but they are composites. And there are a few running stories in this book to elucidate many of the themes and strategies. Of course, I very much hope that you'll see yourself and your child in those characters and stories.

For some readers, the ideas in this book may be familiar. Others may find the ideas to be fairly novel. You may read some things that don't square with your current ways of thinking, and the strategies may seem a bit foreign to you. But let the ideas percolate a little and give the strategies a try, more than once or twice—there's a pretty decent chance they'll grow on you.

Ross Greene
Portland, Maine

- *Chapter 1* -

ROLE CONFUSION

It seems like it's always been this way. Adults telling kids what to do and making them do it. Might makes right. Father knows best. Spare the rod and spoil the child. Do as I say, not as I do. Children should be seen and not heard.

And yet, along with some other historically subjugated groups—women, people of color—children have come a long way. Not so long ago, children were brought into the world to ensure the survival of the species, to help out on the farm, to generate some income, or simply because birth control wasn't yet in vogue or reliable. Nowadays, with the species more populous than ever and with most kids off the hook (in the Western world, anyway) for tending the flock or contributing income, kids have choices. They're real people. They matter. And they know it.

Some observers of Western society are not especially enthusiastic about the rise in kids' status, pointing with alarm at what they perceive as the disrespectful, irreverent character of the modern child (Aristotle, of course, complained about the same thing). They lament the "adultification" of children and look with disdain upon parents who aren't sufficiently in charge. They long for the good old days, when roles were clear, kids knew their place, and administering a well-deserved thrashing wouldn't get you reported to the authorities.

On the other hand, there are those who aren't quite convinced that the good old days were as marvelous as advertised. They've come to realize that might and right don't overlap seamlessly, and that father didn't always know best. They now recognize that the rod was an unnecessary and even counterproductive teaching tool, that thrashings were a pretty extreme way to make a point, and that there's more to raising a kid than carrots and sticks. They believe that allowing children to have a voice in their own affairs might actually be good preparation for The Real World.

So, as it relates to how to raise kids, a lot of parents are a little confused about how to proceed these days. They're mired in that muddy territory that lies between permissiveness and authoritarianism. They want their kid to be independent, but not if he's going to make bad choices. They want to avoid being harsh and rigid, but not if the result is a noncompliant, disrespectful kid. They want to avoid being too pushy and overbearing, but not if an unmotivated, apathetic kid is what they have to show for it. They want to have a good relationship with their kid, but not if that means being a pushover. They don't want to scream, but they do want to be heard.

It's all about balance, but the balance sometimes seems so precarious, so difficult to achieve.

Fortunately, it's not mud that lies between the Dictatorial Kingdom and the Pushover Provinces. It's a partnership, and one in which collaboration, rather than power, is the key ingredient. A partnership that will help you and your kid work together as allies—as teammates—rather than as adversaries. A partnership that will help you forge a relationship that works for both of you, that gives you both room to grow, that provides your child with the solid foundation he needs to someday spread his wings and fly.

We seem to be moving pretty fast here. A collaborative partnership? With my kid? For real?

For real. You may not be aware of it, but you started collaborating with your kid the instant he came into this world. When he cried, you tried to figure out what was the matter. Then you tried to do something about it. Then, based on his feedback, if it became apparent that your intuition or your intervention wasn't spot-on, you adjusted. So you've had a collaborative partnership with your kid for quite some time.

Will I still be an authority figure in a collaborative partnership?

Yes, very much so. Not an "old school" authority figure, but an authority figure nonetheless.

It turns out that what you're mostly looking for, as a parent, is *influence*. Not control. And there is more than one way to get that influence. One path involves power and coercion, but there's another path, one that enhances communication, improves relationships, and better prepares kids for a lot of what actually lies ahead in The Real World. This book, as you might have guessed, is about the second path.

The good news is that, by mere virtue of your position as parent, you already have influence. The bad news is that you don't have as much influence as you thought and that if you use your influence in the wrong way, you'll have even less.

Now some more good news: your child wants influence too.

That's good news?

Yes, that's very good news. For your child to do well in The Real World, he'll need to know what he wants. Of course, it wouldn't be ideal for you to give him everything he wants just because he wants it. So he'll also need to know how to pursue what he wants adaptively and in a way that takes others' needs and concerns into account. As a pretty influential guy named Hillel once wrote, "If I am not for myself, who will be for me? And if I am only for myself, what am I?" The problem, of course, is that Hillel didn't give us the recipe for balancing those two considerations. Nonetheless, you're on the hook for helping your child do it.

Creating a collaborative partnership with a child is unfamiliar territory for many parents, and we adults often aren't very enthusiastic about treading into unfamiliar territory. If we're going to err, it's often going to be in the direction of authoritarianism and rigidity, and we can easily find support for this position, perhaps from parenting experts (depending on who we follow), perhaps in scripture (if we're selective about where we look). But working toward a collaborative partnership has the potential to make parenting far more rewarding and to have you someday looking in the rearview mirror with great satisfaction.

We humans have come so far in so many realms. We have electricity and iPods and smartphones and the Internet. We can communicate instantaneously with people anywhere in the world. We've mastered flight. We've landed people on the moon and explored planets. We can transplant hearts and livers and faces and replace limbs. We can prevent and cure diseases. We can make babies without need of intercourse . . . and help them survive if they're born many months before term.

But we're still overreliant on power and control to solve problems. In that very important respect, we haven't come far enough. And it begins with how we raise our children.

Completing the quote from Hillel, "If not now, when?"

· · · · ·

As you read in the introduction, there are several stories that run throughout the book. Each focuses on a different family. These families' situations will help elucidate the themes and strategies you'll learn about. Let's meet our first family now.

Denise was in her early-morning single-mom frazzle. Three kids to get out the door to school, a job to get to (preferably on time), and a boss who tried to be understanding but didn't take kindly to late-arriving employees.

"Hank, get down here and eat your breakfast! Nick, stop doing your homework and go get dressed for school—you should've finished it last night, anyway! Charlotte, *please* turn off the TV and get your backpack ready. You're going to miss the bus! I've told you a million times not to watch TV in the morning before school! And the dog *still* hasn't been fed!"

Charlotte, the youngest of Denise's kids, meandered into the kitchen. "Can't somebody else be the one who feeds the dog in the morning? There's too much for me to do."

"Fine, I'll feed the dog," said Denise, pouring milk into a bowl of cereal for Hank. "Just get out of here so you don't miss your bus! I don't have time to drive you to school again!"

"I like when you drive me to school," said Charlotte, sitting down on a kitchen chair.

"Charlotte, don't sit down!" said Denise. "I like driving you to school, too, but not when I'm this late. Go!"

Charlotte got up from the chair, just in time for her older brother, Hank, to flick her ear as he sat down for breakfast.

"Mom!"

"Hank, leave her be!" hissed Denise. "What did I tell you was going to happen to your Xbox if you keep torturing your sister?"

"What's for breakfast?" mumbled Hank, still half asleep.

Denise placed the bowl of cereal in front of Hank.

"I don't want cereal," grumbled Hank.

"It's all I have time for today."

"Then I won't eat breakfast."

"There are some frozen waffles in the freezer," offered Denise. "Does that work?"

"I don't want breakfast."

"I don't want you going to school without breakfast," said Denise, opening a can of dog food.

"Yeah, well, I'm not hungry. You never have time to make pancakes except on the weekend."

Hank got up from the table and left the kitchen.

"I can't make pancakes every day!" called Denise. "And nobody else likes pancakes, anyway. Nick, stop with the homework. Do you want the cereal Hank isn't eating?"

"Hank probably got his spit in it already," said Nick.

"That's right, loser," called Hank from the hallway. "'Cuz losers eat my spit."

"I'm not eating it," announced Nick.

Denise sighed and dumped the cereal in the sink and poured a new bowl of cereal for Nick.

"I'm not using the same bowl he spit in!"

"Fine. I'll give you a new bowl." Denise poured fresh cereal and milk into a different bowl and set the dog food in front of Nick.

"This is disgusting!" Nick protested before Denise noticed her error.

"Oh geez!" Denise replaced the dog food with the bowl of cereal.

"Don't spill it on my homework!" Nick warned.

"Bye," Charlotte called from the front hallway.

"Bye, sweetie; I love you!" called Denise.

A minute later, Denise heard Hank leave without saying good-bye. Then she noticed that Nick hadn't touched his cereal.

"Nick, enough with the freaking homework!"

When Nick had left and Denise was finally on her way to work, a few minutes late as usual, she wondered why every morning had to be just like the last. Would it ever get easier?

- Chapter 2 -

INCOMPATIBILITY

As you've already read, every kid has the same task: figure out who she is—her skills, preferences, beliefs, values, personality traits, goals, and direction—get comfortable with it, and then pursue and live a life that is congruent with it. This is what the renowned psychologist Carl Rogers referred to as *self-actualization*.

As you also read, you as a parent have an important task as well: you, too, have to figure out who your child is, get comfortable with it, and then help her live a life that is congruent with it. Notice that it's not your task to mold the lump of clay (your child) into the form you envisioned: she's not a lump of clay, and you don't have that kind of power.

But you also want your kid to benefit from your experience, wisdom, and values. In other words, you want to have influence. That influence is exerted through your *expectations*, which include many realms: *family member* (e.g., chores, how family members should be treated), *health* (hygiene, sleep, food choices), *student* (grades, effort, work habits), *member of society* (how to treat other people, abiding by laws, responsibility to the community at large), and *out-*

comes (being able to earn a living, function independently). Your expectations can't be blind, though; they must be matched to your child's skills, preferences, beliefs, values, personality traits, goals, and direction (summarized hereafter as *characteristics*). And you're not the only one with expectations for your child; the world has academic, social, and behavioral expectations too.

Throughout your child's development, there is a continuous interplay between her characteristics and your and the world's demands and expectations. The bar is continuously raised; the demands and expectations become more intense and complex as your child grows. And your child's characteristics evolve over time as well.

Most kids are able to meet most of the expectations that are placed upon them most of the time. But every kid struggles to meet expectations sometimes, some more than others. In other words, there are times when there is *incompatibility* between your child's characteristics and the demands and expectations that are being placed upon her.

For example, if a classroom teacher insists that your child pay rapt attention and sit still for long periods of time and your child is distractible and hyperactive, or finds much of the material less than captivating, then there's incompatibility between the teacher's expectations and your child's characteristics. Now, if your child is driven to succeed against all odds, or is eager to please, or has the ability to muster the psychic energy to focus even when she's bored stiff, or if she's fearful of your wrath in response to bad grades, she may be able to overcome the distractibility, hyperactivity, and/or boredom, at least some of the time. But if your child does not possess any or many of these characteristics, the incompatibility will remain.

INCOMPATIBILITY

If the peers on your child's school bus are boisterous and tease a lot and your child is very quiet, shy, and sensitive, there may be incompatibility between the social demands on the school bus and your child's capacity to respond effectively. If your child has the ability to let things roll off her back, or if she's able to join up with other kids who are equally introverted, she may be able to reduce or even surmount the incompatibility on the school bus. But if she doesn't possess these protective characteristics and isn't able to transcend the incompatibility on the school bus, it will remain.

There's also incompatibility if your child's teacher is assigning massive quantities of math homework and your child only marginally understands the material and is therefore having difficulty completing that homework. If your child is tenacious in response to adversity, or has the wherewithal to seek assistance when she needs it and the persistence to seek help elsewhere if the initial help isn't helpful—or if the teacher is very attuned to his or her students, good at noticing when kids are struggling, and highly skilled at providing help—your child may be able to overcome the incompatibility. Otherwise, the incompatibility will remain.

Notice that, in the last example, dealing with incompatibility isn't the sole responsibility of your kid. Sometimes a kid needs a partner to help out. And one of your most important roles as a partner is that of *helper*.

We tend to limit our use of the word *helper* to those in professional roles—physicians, mental health professionals, educators—but as a parent, you're in one of the helping professions too. That being the case, there are probably some things you should know about being a helper:

11

1. *Helpers help.* In other words, helpers abide by the Hippocratic Oath, which goes something like this: *don't make things worse.*
2. *Helpers have thick skin.* In other words, they try hard not to take things too personally. That way, they can stay as objective as possible and maintain their perspective. While helpers are entitled to their own feelings, they aren't ruled by them. In other words, helpers try very hard to make sure that their own feelings don't interfere with helping.
3. *Helpers only help when their help is really needed.* That way, helpers also promote independence.

Sticking with these themes can be tough. There's no love like the love parents feel for their children. You've been caring for and worrying about that kid for a long time. You were there when she was totally dependent on you as an infant, and you've been there through thick and thin ever since. Parenting has provided you with some of the best times of your life.

And also some of the worst, which can make it hard to stay in helping mode, or cause you to try helping in ways that are incongruent with your role as a partner. But maintaining that role is what you're striving for. Even when your kid doesn't meet your expectations. Even when your kid says things that are hurtful. Even when, perhaps during adolescence, your kid acts like she doesn't want to have anything to do with you anymore. Even when it becomes clear that you're no longer as appealing to hang out with as her peers. You're still a partner.

Life is far less stressful—and your child doesn't need a partner quite so much—when there's compatibility between her characteristics and the world's demands and expectations. It's incompatibility—*struggling*—that stresses kids and parents out and that sets the stage for a variety of disadvantageous responses in both kids and their caregivers.

Yet, it's also incompatibility that is the impetus for growth and resilience.

In other words, incompatibility isn't all bad. In fact, incompatibility can be very good. Which is good, because incompatibility is inevitable. The conflict that often accompanies incompatibility isn't good. Or necessary.

Seeing your kid struggle isn't fun. The trick is to pay close attention to whether she needs your help to overcome incompatibility or can manage it on her own. And the magic is in how, if she does need your help, you handle things from there.

IN THE BEGINNING
· · · · ·

Let's rewind the tape a little. The interface between your child's characteristics and the world's expectations began the instant she was born. What demands are placed on infants? Without being exhaustive—and recognizing that expectations vary across families and kids—there are demands for self-soothing, regulating and modulating emotions, ingesting and digesting food, establishing a regular sleep cycle, adapting to the sensory world (heat, cold, lights, noises, changes, etc.), perhaps sleeping in a separate bed, and interacting with people (in fairly rudimentary ways early on, with rapidly increasing sophistication as she gets older). If, in infancy, a child has the skills to handle these demands without great difficulty, then, all other things being equal, there is compatibility and things are likely to go fairly smoothly. But if a kid lacks the skills to handle these expectations—has what's often referred to as a difficult temperament—or if the expectations of the environment are out of whack, then there is incompatibility and a heightened risk for things to go less smoothly.

How do infants communicate that there is incompatibility? Since words are not an option, they do it by crying, screaming, turning red in the face, thrashing about, vomiting, hyperventilating, sleeping too little or too much, and so forth. If caregivers have difficulty interpreting and being responsive to these signs, the incompatibility will likely be heightened.

Of course, infancy is just the beginning of the compatibility/incompatibility journey, of the never-ending interplay between expectations and a child's characteristics. There are many points in development—we might call them *points of vulnerability*—at which incompatibility could arise. For example, during the toddler years, the world starts demanding that kids begin expressing their needs, thoughts, and concerns in *words*. When children start "using their words" in accordance with expectations, there's compatibility. When children do not develop language processing and communication skills in accordance with expectations, or if the demands and expectations are out of whack, then there's incompatibility.

In addition to language, another emerging skill kicks in at around twelve to eighteen months: *locomotion*. Language and locomotion are exciting developments, but they can also contribute to incompatibility. See, long before these skills emerge, children already have some pretty clear ideas about what they want and when they want it (usually *right now!*), but language and locomotion are what set the stage for them to *go for it*. In one respect—especially as it relates to a child starting to figure out who she is, get comfortable with it, and pursue a life that is congruent with it—knowing what she wants and going for it is a good thing. But because what she wants and when she wants it may not be feasible or safe, parental influence is really important.

How do toddlers communicate that there is incompatibility? Often with the universal sign of incompatibility: the tantrum. Regrettably, tantrums have given a bad name—the terrible twos—to this exciting time in a child's development. But the last thing you'd want to do is view early expressions of your child's skills, preferences, beliefs, values, personality traits, goals, and direction as a terrible thing. Tantrums are simply a signal that there's incompatibility, not a sign that your child is challenging your desire to have influence. Tantrums let you know that your child needs some help sorting things through and that it's time to get the ball rolling on teaching and modeling some important developmental skills such as delay of gratification, expressing concerns in an adaptive manner, taking into account the concerns and needs of other people, frustration tolerance, flexibility, and problem-solving. Tantrums are not an indication that your child needs massive doses of Who's the Boss. If you play your cards right, the terrible twos can be a time of tremendous growth, learning, and exploration. The same can be said for the tumultuous threes. And the fearsome fours. And everything that comes after.

Speaking of what comes after, when children reach the age of three or four, the world starts demanding that they sit still and pay attention for rather lengthy periods of time, that they demonstrate greater flexibility and adaptability, and that they exhibit increasingly sophisticated, nuanced social skills. Sustained attention and self-regulation are among the broad constellation of skills known as *executive functions*, which are integrally related to a kid's ability to solve problems, handle frustration effectively, adapt, make decisions, plan, control impulses, and reflect on past experience and bring it to bear in the present. *Social skills* represent an equally broad category that includes other skills such as sharing, entering a group, starting a conversation, and asserting oneself appropriately, along with more sophisticated, crucial skills such as empathy, appreciating how one's behavior is affecting others, and taking another's perspective. Countless additional expectations—some more mundane than others—are placed on kids throughout childhood: potty training; going to and staying in bed at night; getting ready for school in a timely manner; dressing independently; separating from caregivers; mastering spelling, writing, math, reading, and homework; participating in sports; making and keeping friends; and settling disagreements adaptively. Of course, that list barely scratches the surface. Yet the refrain is the same: when a kid is able to meet those expectations, there is compatibility; when a kid has difficulty meeting those expectations, there is incompatibility.

How do older kids communicate that there is incompatibility? As they did when they were younger, through their behavior: pouting, sulking, withdrawing, screaming, swearing, throwing things, slamming doors, lying, or skipping school. At the extreme end of the spectrum, kids may communicate that there is incompatibility by exhibiting behaviors that are injurious to themselves or others, such as hitting, destroying property, cutting, self-induced vomiting, using alcohol or drugs to excess, and worse. And there are many other possible indicators of incompatibility, such as poor grades, lack of interest in school, having few or no friends, excessive use of video games, and so forth.

INCOMPATIBILITY

Adults have a tendency to concentrate too heavily on the *signs* of incompatibility, typically a kid's *behavior*. Many mental health professionals have the same inclination. But *behavior is just the means by which your child communicates that there is incompatibility*. It's the fever—the signal. To have influence, *you'll need to see beyond the behavior and focus on identifying and solving the problems that are causing it*. Behavior is what's going on *downstream*. You want to focus *upstream*, on resolving the incompatibilities that are causing the behavior.

If a child exhibits enough maladaptive behaviors enough of the time, then there's an excellent chance she will meet criteria for one or more of the categories that many mental health professionals rely upon for rendering psychiatric diagnoses, which, in general, comprise long lists of undesirable behaviors. We could debate the pros and cons of childhood psychiatric diagnoses—in the interest of full disclosure, I find that they often do more harm than good—but one thing is certain: while a diagnosis certifies that there is incompatibility, it also implies that the source of the incompatibility is the *child* and therefore increases the likelihood that adults will be focused on *fixing the problem child* rather than on *improving compatibility*.

By the way, there are lots of kids who are struggling but don't meet diagnostic criteria for any particular psychiatric disorder. So you wouldn't want to wait for a psychiatric diagnosis to be rendered before concluding that there is incompatibility.

Even when diagnoses aren't being applied, many of the adjectives that are commonly invoked to characterize kids who aren't meeting expectations also imply that the problem resides within the kid: unmotivated, lazy, weak, manipulative, intransigent, willful, attention seeking, limit testing, disrespectful, to name a few. These characterizations often give rise to many of the erroneous things we say about kids who aren't meeting expectations. Here's a partial list:

"She enjoys doing poorly."
"She enjoys pushing my buttons."
"She thinks she can pull the wool over my eyes."
"She doesn't care."
"She's just a bad seed."
"She's not working up to her potential."
"I know she can do it . . . the effort's just not there."
"She needs to wake up."
"Somebody needs to light a fire under that kid."
"It looks like she's going to have to hit rock bottom before she'll want to float."

These terms and expressions also cause parents to focus on *fixing the problem child* rather than on *improving compatibility*.

YOU
· · · · ·

Let's talk about you a little. You presumably have a wide range of strong emotions tied up in that kid of yours. You want to be a good parent. You want to do it right. You want your child to feel loved, cared for, and protected. You want to make sure she turns out OK. You want to make sure she's ready for The Real World. Maybe you want to parent in ways that are similar to the ways you were parented. Or perhaps you're determined to do things differently.

INCOMPATIBILITY

All parents bring a variety of tendencies and characteristics to the compatibility/incompatibility equation. Here are some of the most important:

- how attuned and responsive you are to your child and her needs
- how you handle stress and frustration
- your level of resilience
- your level of patience
- what you need from your relationship with your child
- the type of relationship you envisioned having with your child
- what you envisioned it would be like to be a parent
- the manner in which you relate to and interact with your child
- how much time you want to spend together
- how much you actually enjoy hanging out with your child
- the extent to which you are pulled away from parenting by work or other distractions
- your awareness of how *your* behavior is affecting hers
- your sensitivity to whether the expectations you're placing on your child are reasonable and realistic

As you may have experienced firsthand, kids are not the only ones at risk for being harshly characterized when there's incompatibility. Society reserves its harshest judgments for their parents: they're inconsistent, passive, lax, permissive, rigid, not rigid enough, namby-pamby, coddling, overinvolved, underinvolved, overprotective, hovering, indifferent, irresponsible. But viewing parents as "the problem" is as counterproductive as viewing the child as "the problem," and simply points us toward *fixing the problem parent* rather than toward *improving compatibility*.

THE CONFLUENCE
· · · · ·

Now we can begin to bring the different forces together: your *child*, with her characteristics; *you*, with your expectations; and the *world*, with demands and expectations of its own. We know that those forces sometimes produce compatibility, sometimes incompatibility. We've also established that the manner in which you respond when there is incompatibility is what will determine whether you and your child are partners, whether you're being an effective helper, and whether your influence is truly influential.

Q & A

Question: How did my child get her characteristics? Is it primarily nature or nurture?

Answer: It's primarily, and always, both. Her skills—and yours, too—are influenced 100 percent by nature and 100 percent by nurture.

There's the temptation to think of some characteristics, such as those caused by genetic disorders, as solely determined by nature. But the field of epigenetics tells us that while a child might be genetically predisposed to a particular disorder, there are a variety of nongenetic factors that determine whether the gene will be activated. Indeed, nurture— for example, the mother's level of stress and the substances, good and bad, that she puts in her body during pregnancy—is exerting influence in utero, and even before the child is conceived. And the environment continues to affect the child's outcome throughout her life.

There's also the temptation to think of some characteristics as purely determined by environmental factors. There's no question that trauma, neglect, poverty, family dysfunction, and other environmental risk factors can *contribute to* or *exacerbate* certain characteristics, but they don't *cause* those characteristics. That's why kids from the same tough neighborhood or family situation can have completely different characteristics. It's why kids who have endured similar traumatic experiences have vastly different reactions to and outcomes following those experiences.

The reality is that your child is a composite of myriad characteristics, and those characteristics are influenced by a *symphony* of environmental and genetic factors. There are no simple explanations for how a kid turns out, though it feels more efficient to pretend that there are. "She's vertically challenged because her mother smoked when she was pregnant" would be too simple. "She's misbehaving because her parents are incompetent disciplinarians" would be incomplete as well. "There's trouble in that kid's gene pool going back a long way." Perhaps so, but now you know there's more to it than that.

Question: Are "expectations" and "rules" the same thing?
Answer: They are roughly synonymous, but the term *expectations* is preferable. When kids "break the rules," adults tend

to respond in a rigid, punitive manner, so as to compel the following of the rules. But when kids are having "difficulty meeting expectations," the range of potential responses—as you'll soon see—expands greatly.

Question: Aren't there some expectations my kid just *has* to meet?
Answer: There certainly are some expectations you very badly want your kid to meet. But if those expectations are incompatible with her characteristics, then simply trying harder to make her meet those expectations is only likely to increase the level of incompatibility and move you further away from a partnership.

Question: How early can I begin partnering with my child?
Answer: Again, you began responding to incompatibility when your child was an infant. Your response was influenced by how attuned you were to what your infant was communicating (since she had no words) and how reliable and attentive you were to her needs. Did she need movement to fall asleep? Was she easily startled or awakened by noise? What was the best timing for feeding? Did she want to be held a lot? Did she have a strong preference for sleeping near you?

Yes, being responsive and reliable requires an enormous amount of time, energy, and commitment. When you decided to be a parent, you simultaneously decided to put someone else (your kid) first for a while. That's what you signed up for. Those first three years of your child's life do set the stage for much of the development that occurs later, so stimulation—not in the form of a video screen but rather in the form of your face, voice, presence, time, involvement, and attention—is a big deal. You don't need to be too concerned about giving your infant or toddler too much attention and love.

Is infancy the ideal time to teach your child that the world isn't always a reliable and responsive place? No—she has plenty of time to learn about that, and she needs a reliable, responsive foundation far more than she needs you to provide early lessons on how unreliable and unresponsive the world can be. In other words, she needs solid roots before she can start spreading her wings.

Question: This idea that incompatibility is a good thing— can you say more about that?

Answer: Expanding on the work of Erik Erikson, the noted psychologist James Marcia has written extensively about the four potential outcomes of your child's journey, depending on the degree to which she has (a) actively explored alternative identities and (b) actually committed to a particular identity or self-concept (skills, beliefs, values, preferences, personality traits, goals, and direction):

- *Identity foreclosure* refers to a person who has not gone through the process of exploring her identity or self-concept but rather has blindly accepted the identity that was provided to or imposed upon her in childhood by parents and other significant caregivers. While this person has committed to an identity, the commitment is not a result of her own searching. An example of this might be a person who chooses a certain profession and lifestyle based on parental expectations but who might have gone in a completely different direction had she had the opportunity to explore and get comfortable with her identity.

- *Identity moratorium* refers to a person who is still actively searching for an identity but has yet to make commitments to specific beliefs, values, preferences, and goals. An example of this might be a person who shuffled between eight different majors while in college but never settled on one and now moves frequently from one job to another. She's still exploring and searching for her identity.

- *Identity diffusion* refers to a person who has neither attempted to explore her identity nor made any commitments to specific values and beliefs. This person may be depressed or apathetic, for she has no idea who or what she is, where she belongs, or where she's heading. She may even turn to negative activities, such as crime or drugs, as it is sometimes easier to slip into a negative identity than to have none at all.

- *Identity achievement* refers to a person who has both undergone the identity exploration process and has also developed a well-defined self-concept and identity. She knows who she is, what she believes, and where she's going.

According to Dr. Marcia, what prompts an individual to begin the self-exploration process that is at the heart of searching for one's identity? Typically, it is *grappling with a crisis* that gets the ball rolling: for example, the death of a close relative or friend, moving to a new town, attending a new school, being rejected by one's friends, not being admitted to the school of one's choice, struggling academically, enduring a romantic breakup, getting arrested, losing or being dissatisfied with one's job, or experiencing financial pressures. In other words, *struggling is often what precedes growth*. Interestingly, the ingredient central to a lot of struggling is—wait for it—*incompatibility*. As David Brooks tells us in his book *The Road to Character*, each struggle leaves a residue; a person who goes through these struggles is more substantial and deep as a result.

Is it your role as a parent to *create* incompatibility to ensure that your kid grows, develops beliefs and values, sets goals, recognizes her strengths and vulnerabilities, and moves in a direction? No. There's no need to manufacture incompatibility; it's inevitable. Should you feel responsible for ensuring that life goes as smoothly as possible for your child so as to remove all potential for incompatibility? No. It would be equally counterproductive to go overboard on removing the bumps from the road. In a competitive world, can you really afford to let her stumble? In a competitive world, she'd better know how to get back on her feet when she stumbles, because you won't always be there to lend a hand.

Question: I think I'm OK with everything I've read so far, but I didn't realize I needed to give so much thought to being a parent. I don't think my parents thought this much about parenting me. They weren't perfect, but I turned out OK. Do I really need to think this much? Am I really trying to be the perfect parent?

Answer: The goal isn't to be the perfect parent, especially since that goal is unachievable. Nor is the goal to second-guess every parenting decision. The goal is to think about your role in your child's life, how to best have influence, and how to foster the characteristics you value most.

Question: It seems like the world is demanding things of kids earlier and earlier in development. Do you agree?

Answer: I do. Apparently, we need to keep up with the Joneses. And not only the Joneses, but also the Finns (as in the people of Finland), because their schoolchildren are doing better than ours on academic testing and achievement these days. Of course, when we get carried away with our expectations—when we push the developmental envelope on expectations—we increase the likelihood of incompatibility. Many kids seem to be rising to the challenge of the intensified timeline on skills (though at the cost of being more anxious and stressed out), but it's quite apparent that an increasing number aren't.

· · · · ·

We've covered a lot of ground in this chapter. Before we meet another family, here's a summary of the key themes you've just read about:

- Your child's task—and yours as well—is to figure out who she is, get comfortable with it, and then pursue and live a life that is congruent with it. But you also want to have influence, based on your experience, wisdom, and values. Maintaining that balance is the challenge.

- Your influence is exerted through your expectations. When your child is able to meet those expectations, there is compatibility; when she's unable to, there's incompatibility.

- The manner in which you go about responding to that incompatibility will have a significant impact on your relationship with your child, how well you communicate with one another, and whether your influence is truly influential.

- Incompatibility isn't a bad thing; it's what fuels most growth. It's also unavoidable.

· · · · ·

Dan Fessinger's day finally ended at 8:30 p.m. He was a partner in a small but busy law firm, and he'd been in meetings and a deposition for seven consecutive hours. He spent a good portion of his very long days battling adversarial attorneys, but it was the path he had chosen as a litigator. As he prepared to leave the office, he looked at his cell phone and saw six missed calls from his wife, Kristin. He rolled his eyes. "Gotta be about Taylor," he grumbled, referring to their sixteen-year-old daughter. "Do I have the energy for this right now?"

Dan had two older kids from a prior marriage and had a good relationship with them. He had a pretty good relationship with Taylor, too, though she was more prickly and temperamental than his older children had been. But his nonconfrontational disposition outside of the office was at odds with Kristin's notions about the role he should be playing in Taylor's life. She often implored him to support her in reining in their daughter, who'd been a handful since birth. "I don't want her to split us," Kristin said frequently. "We need to be on the same page." These days, Taylor was far more communicative with Dan than with Kristin.

Dan settled into his car for the ride home and sighed as he mustered the energy to call his wife.

"Geez, you're just like Taylor!" Kristin exclaimed when she answered the phone. "You don't answer your cell phone either! Where have you been?"

"I haven't had a break since one p.m. Taylor's not answering her phone?"

"No," said Kristin. "I don't know where she is."

"Well, she could be at the library," Dan offered.

"She's not at the library!" scoffed Kristin. "She never answers her cell phone when she sees it's me calling. She's probably at Scott's house." Scott was a friend of Taylor's. "And I bet his parents aren't home."

"Did you try calling his house?"

"No answer there either. Geez, this pisses me off! I don't know where she is half the time!"

"She has a decent head on her shoulders," said Dan, wincing at the anticipated response.

"She does not have a good head on her shoulders, Dan! That's why I have to watch her like a hawk!"

Dan was tempted to suggest that watching Taylor like a hawk probably explained why she didn't answer Kristin's calls, but thought better of it. *This is like dancing on a tightrope*, he thought to himself. *Rebellious daughter, high-strung, anxious wife. Seven straight hours of meetings is a walk in the park compared to this.* "I guess she'll show up soon."

"So that's it? She'll show up soon?"

"I'm not sure what you want me to say."

"I saw a story on the news tonight. There's an app that will let me shut down her cell phone if she doesn't answer my calls. I'm installing it. And I'm grounding her."

Great, thought Dan. *So all the strong-arming that's led us here will be fixed with more strong-arming.*

INCOMPATIBILITY

Kristin was looking for an endorsement, not silence. "We have to be on the same page," she demanded. "What do you say?"

Whose page? Dan thought. "To tell you the truth, my mind is kind of numb right now," said Dan. "Any chance we can talk about this after I've had some dinner?"

"You better get home and eat quick," said Kristin. "'Cuz it's not going to be pretty when that kid walks through the door."

Chapter 3

BUSINESS AS USUAL

How would one go about trying to fix a problem child? Let us count the ways! But before we do, let's consider the thinking that gives rise to those options.

When kids struggle to meet our expectations, many adults react with a common bias: the tendency to assume that *all things are possible with sufficient effort.* Flowing from this bias is a related one: *if my child isn't meeting a particular expectation, it must be because he isn't motivated to devote sufficient effort to the cause.* And there's one more: *my child's failure to meet expectations reflects badly on me as his parent.*

These biases cause adults to respond to kids who are having difficulty meeting expectations by exhorting or extorting them to put forth greater effort, which is a far cry from *improving compatibility.* Let's see what exhorting and extorting might look like:

Simply point out to the child that he's not meeting a given expectation.

Parent: Sam, I'm concerned about the grade you received this semester in math. You really need to do better.

There's certainly nothing wrong with reminding your child of your expectations and making sure he's aware that he's falling short. Some kids respond to this strategy by redoubling their focus or effort, and things improve. But for many kids, simple reminders don't get the job done. The litmus test here is fairly straightforward: if you're frequently reminding your kid of a particular expectation, then reminding isn't working. No reason to think additional reminding—perhaps in the form of nagging or badgering—will get the job done. Maybe Sam just doesn't appreciate why it's so important that he do well in math . . .

Explain why it's important that he meet the expectation.
This strategy involves communicating your wisdom and experience to your child.

Parent: Sam, it's really important that you keep up in math—what you're learning now is the foundation for what you'll be learning next semester.

Sam: I know.

He knows? If he already knows, then explaining it again won't accomplish the mission. Maybe he needs a push . . .

Push (insist that the child meet the expectation).
Parent: Well, you're going to have to do better than this.

Sam: I know. I'm trying. It's really hard.

Insisting harder—which can occur in a variety of forms, including counting to three—is an extremely popular way of responding to kids who are having difficulty meeting an expectation. And, on occasion, some kids actually respond to insisting harder. But many don't. In fact, some respond badly. We know this because of the challenging behaviors they begin to exhibit in response to unrelenting insisting (and counting). We also may have missed the hint Sam gave us, something about the math being really hard. *We were too consumed with ensuring that the expectation was met.* Maybe he needs some energy . . .

Pump him up.

Parent: Come on! I know you can do it! You're really smart!

Gotta love the enthusiasm and optimism. Sometimes adding enthusiasm and optimism to the mix is helpful. But often it is not, because these ingredients probably *won't address the true factors accounting for Sam's poor performance in math.*

Knock him down.

Parent: Geez, this is getting a little ridiculous! I don't know what I need to do to get you to do better in math! I know you can do it; I've seen you do it before. Get your act together!

The fact that Sam has, *on occasion*, been able to do the math is now being introduced as evidence that Sam should *always* be able to do the math. But since it's quite clear that Sam *usually* has *difficulty* with the math, it's not exactly clear why we'd expect him to be able to do it *without* difficulty *most of the time.* Still, let's keep going. Maybe it's time for you to take over . . .

Solve the problem for the child.

Parent: Well, then you're going to have to stay after school so Mrs. D'Angelo can give you extra help.

Sam: I've been to her for extra help! She doesn't help me!

Imposing a solution might seem like a perfectly reasonable approach. It certainly is a common one. But imposed solutions are usually just shots in the dark, since *we still have no idea what's getting in the way for Sam in math*. If you're shooting for durable, effective solutions, it's helpful to know what you're aiming at.

But let's say Sam goes along with his parent's solution. Let's listen in a few months later when the next report card comes home:

Parent: Sam, you're still not doing well in math.

Sam: I know. I still don't get it.

Looks like the parent's solution didn't work. That's not a catastrophe, but as you'll soon see, it may have been predictable. Unilateral solutions have a very high crash-and-burn rate. What comes next?

Consequences, Part I: Rewards

Parent: How 'bout if you pull your math grade up to a B this semester, we get you that video game you've been wanting? What's it called?

Sam: Assassin's Creed?

Parent: Whaddya think?!

Sam: I always wanted Assassin's Creed!

Sam sure does want that video game. Of course, we still don't have the slightest idea about what's getting in his way in math. While a highly desirable incentive has the potential to improve performance temporarily, there's a decent chance—you may have experienced this firsthand already—that it's not going to solve the problem durably.

Now what? Well, you do have other options in the consequences department . . .

Consequences, Part II: Punishment

Parent: Sam, I've tried everything I can do to help you in math! You don't want Mrs. D'Angelo's help, so I tried helping you myself. I even offered to buy you a video game if you improved your grade. Nothing's working. So if your math grade doesn't come up to a B this semester, I'm taking away all of your video games.

Sam: That's not fair!

Punishments, just like rewards, have the potential to improve performance temporarily, but often not durably. They also have the potential to significantly increase the level of conflict between you and your child. Many parents instinctively and instantaneously apply punishments whenever their child is having difficulty meeting an expectation, as if they have no other options.

Of course, many of the aforementioned strategies can be delivered more harshly, with screaming, threatening, berating, and additional disparaging, in the misguided belief that *increased intensity* will improve the likelihood that the message will get through. You not only lose "style points" by adding these ingredients, but you also increase the speed at which you lose your kid.

Lose my kid? I'm just trying to do what's best for him.

Perhaps so, but what's best for him is likely to involve more "listening" than "lessoning." And—this is definitely worth pointing out—*the message has already gotten through*: Sam knows, and has known for quite some time, that his parents want him to do well in math.

But what about "tough love"?

Parents who say they're practicing "tough love" have a tendency to emphasize the "tough" part far more than the "love" part. And while love is a wonderful thing, it's not going to solve the problem.

Many parents stick with these popular strategies for a long time. They keep insisting that the child meet a given expectation. They say they're at their wit's end. They add and take away privileges. They punish. They spank. They say they don't know what else to do.

These strategies are often ineffective—and even counterproductive—or some very good reasons. If we're wrong in our belief that Sam's poor performance in math is a sign that he's not devoting sufficient effort to the cause, then interventions aimed at ensuring that he devotes even greater effort to the cause won't accomplish the mission. Indeed, these strategies could make things worse in a variety of ways. After all, Sam's pretty frustrated about doing poorly in math too. Unless he's already given up all hope of doing well in math, in which case he may not be so unhappy about it anymore, and may have stopped trying as well. So adding incentives to the mix—when poor motivation isn't really what's getting in the way—will only cause greater frustration. And Sam's already pretty agitated about the fact that he's not achieving promised rewards and is on the receiving end of various punishments. Unless he's been so overcorrected and overpunished that he's habituated to the stream of natural and adult-imposed consequences that have been flowing his way and is no longer impacted by them. Some overpunished kids simply become resolved to prove to adults that punishment, no matter how severe, has no effect on them whatsoever.

Moreover, many of these strategies represent an effort to *force* a child to meet an expectation, through use of power. Unfortunately, force and power tend to bring out the worst in human beings, both younger (e.g., your child) and older (e.g., you). Worse, if your child has a certain personality . . . or if he's just following your cues . . . or if he can't reliably do what you're forcing him to do . . . he's going to respond to the use of power by asserting whatever power *he* has, resulting in what is commonly known as a power struggle. The primary goal of a power struggle is to figure out who's going to win and who's going to lose—in other words, it's a win-lose proposition. The reality is that no one wins in a power struggle; it just feels like someone's winning because they prevailed, at least for now. Whether that's you or your kid—at least some of the time it'll probably be your kid—the whole scenario is rather pointless.

Pointless?

Yes, pointless. While power is the currency of a power struggle—indeed, it's the currency of the Dictatorial Kingdom—power doesn't solve problems, not durably anyway. Power isn't the currency in the Collaborative Territories; there, you're relying on alternative currencies: *information* and *collaboration*.

Information?

Information is crucial. If we can tear ourselves away from the automatic assumptions that Sam's difficulties in math are rooted in poor effort and motivation . . . if we can instead view Sam's poor performance in math as an indication that there is incompatibility between the demands and expectations of his math class and Sam's characteristics, including his *skills* . . . then it becomes crystal clear why reminding, cheerleading, reassuring, explaining, insisting, badgering, pushing, disparaging, rewarding, punishing, berating, and screaming aren't getting the job done. No matter how much power is applied, until we have the information we need—*What's really getting in the way for Sam in math?*—the problem will remain unsolved.

And collaboration?

Collaboration is crucial too. Adults often try to solve problems by doing something *to* a kid; it's actually a lot more productive to solve problems *with* the kid, as partners.

Finally, these strategies often have the effect of causing a child to look *outside* of himself for the impetus to do the right thing. You don't want your child looking outside of himself for that; you want him looking *inside*. If you *force* your values on your kid, you stand an excellent chance of having them rejected. Having influence means resolving incompatibilities in ways that help him explore his own values and internalize some of yours. Helping your child focus on his inner compass—his own voice—is a much more reliable way to help kids do the right thing. For the reasons just described, punishment can actually *interfere* with helping kids hear that inner voice; often, it's their anger at the punishers—or simply "not getting caught"—that becomes their primary focus.

KEY THEMES
· · · · ·

This seems like a good time to introduce the overarching theme of this entire book:

Kids do well if they can.

This is the belief that if your kid *could* do well, he *would* do well. If your kid isn't doing well—if he's not meeting a given expectation—it's your job to figure out why and to put poor motivation at the bottom of the list. Better yet, take poor motivation off the list completely. Poor motivation is *never* a satisfactory explanation for anything. If you can't figure out why on your own, it's your job to find someone who can help you do it.

Here's a closely related and equally important theme:

Your child would prefer to be doing well.

Society is *set up* to be a rewarding place for those who do well. In general, whatever perceived incentives there are for doing poorly, they are greatly outweighed by the incentives for doing well. The assumption that a child who isn't meeting an expectation must not be motivated to meet that expectation is almost always incorrect. *Skills* are the engine pulling the train; *motivation* is the caboose.

Here's one more:

**Good parenting means being
responsive to the hand you've been dealt.**

At every point along the way, you're going to be concerned with *your* kid and the expectations he is and isn't meeting, whether the expectations he's having difficulty meeting are realistic, and the best ways to balance his characteristics with your wisdom, experience, and values. It's wonderful if someone else's kid is meeting a certain expectation, but that really has very little to do with your kid and the expectations he's having difficulty meeting. While it's easy to be concerned about the cards the other players are holding, when it comes to being responsive to the hand you've been dealt, you and your child will be a lot better off if you focus on your own.

I should mention that the *kids do well if they can* theme can be applied to you as well. It turns out that *parents do well if they can* too.

Q & A

Question: Aren't I, as my child's parent, responsible for how he turns out?

Answer: As you've read, your child didn't come into this world as a blank slate; *he was already somebody when he showed up.* That means you have less control over how your child turns out than you may think. You're responsible for being responsive to the hand you've been dealt, for exerting influence in ways that are truly influential, and for dealing with incompatibility in ways that bring out the best in you and your child.

Question: So adult-imposed consequences are out of the parenting mix completely?

Answer: The big question is whether you really *need* adult-imposed consequences. Sticker charts, privilege gain, privilege loss, time-outs, grounding, and so forth—I sometimes call them *unnatural* or *artificial* consequences—really only accomplish two things: letting your kid know he's not meeting a given expectation (you could probably just tell him, and he probably already knows) and giving him the incentive to meet that expectation (if *kids do well if they can*, then he's already motivated). If something is getting in the way of his meeting that expectation, then you badly need to know what that something is, and consequences don't provide you with that information. In fact, consequences can make information gathering more difficult; kids sometimes clam up if they're worried about your anger or being punished.

I should mention that there are other types of consequences besides the adult-imposed variety. There are also *natural* consequences—poor grades, feeling embarrassed, not being selected for a desired team, and so forth—which tend to be very powerful and very persuasive, and are also unavoidable. The mystery is why so many parents add adult-imposed consequences when it's already clear that those very powerful and persuasive natural consequences aren't getting the job done. Your child needs something else from you.

Question: I feel like the message won't get through if I don't use consequences.

Answer: If the message you're trying to get through is the fact that you have concerns about expectations that aren't being met, and that you really want those concerns to be addressed and really want the problem to get solved, there's another way to help you accomplish that mission. You'll be learning about that other way in the next chapter.

Question: Don't consequences need to be immediate?

Answer: A lot of us were taught that adult-imposed consequences should be immediate so as to make clear the link between a kid's behaviors and the consequences of those behaviors. That often leads to two mistakes: (1) focusing primarily on the kid's behaviors, rather than on the incompatibilities that are causing those behaviors; and (2) rushing to judgment and action. But adult-imposed consequences don't resolve incompatibilities; and resolving incompatibilities is best accomplished proactively rather than emergently. Immediate or not, adult-imposed consequences are unnecessary in most instances and counterproductive in many.

Question: So I shouldn't reward my kid for doing things I want him to do, like chores?

Answer: Not if you're trying to help him understand that pitching in is an important part of being a member of a family. Not if you want him to understand that doing the right thing doesn't always have an extrinsic reward attached to it. And not if you want to understand what's getting in his way if he's having difficulty doing his chores.

Question: I sometimes spank my kids, and I'm starting to think that practice is even more extreme than many of the interventions described in this chapter. Thoughts?

Answer: There is one guiding principle most people can agree on when it comes to disciplining kids: the strategy that is chosen for exerting influence and providing guidance should be the *least toxic response*. Physical punishment is increasingly recognized as the *most toxic response*.

There is now a significant body of research documenting the significant damage done by hitting kids. There is also a diverse array of research-based, effective parenting strategies that are equally or more effective than hitting, and less harmful. Entire nations have come to this recognition: in 1979, Sweden became the first nation to outlaw spanking, and forty-nine countries have since chosen the same path. Many professional groups, including the American Academy of Pediatrics and the American Academy of Child and Adolescent Psychiatry, have called on parents to abandon spanking as a form of punishment.

Yet, UNICEF estimates that throughout the world, one *billion* kids are still on the receiving end of regular physical punishment. In the United States, one-third of kids are hit *before the age of one*, and 80 to 90 percent of toddlers are hit by their parents. These data suggest that parents aren't the only ones experiencing this developmental period as *terrible*. And it's not just in our households that the hitting occurs. In nineteen American states, corporal punishment is still legal and practiced in schools, with hundreds of thousands of paddlings annually.

In the Western world, there are those who point to Judeo-Christian scripture for their justification in hitting children, with the renowned one (Proverbs 13:24)—*Whoever spares the rod hates their children, but the one who loves their children is careful to discipline them*—being the most commonly cited (that one is best known in its paraphrased form, *Spare the rod and spoil the child*, apparently first articulated by Samuel Butler in 1662). But scripture is actually a decidedly mixed bag when it comes to parenting; support for a variety of different parenting practices and beliefs can be found in its contents.

Indeed, there are passages suggesting that a more empathic, individualized approach to parenting might be a good idea. Here are a few, starting with what is commonly known as the Golden Rule:

Do to others as you would have them do to you. (Luke 6:31)

Love your neighbor as yourself. (Leviticus 19:18)

Everyone should be quick to listen, slow to speak and slow to become angry. (James 1:19)

Educate a child according to his path . . . (Proverbs 22:6)

That last one means that every child is an individual and that caregivers are on the hook for finding ways to transmit our experience, wisdom, and values in the ways that are best and most effective for each child. The maxim applies not only to education, where it is actually memorialized in special education law in North America and elsewhere, but also to parenting. In the same way that children learn and must be taught math differently— some take to it more readily than others, and some need extra help—your child's temperament and personality should have significant bearing on how you go about exerting influence.

In the eighteenth century, Elijah Ben Solomon wrote that when a child is small, his parents might be able to impose their will in ways that are contrary to his path but that eventually when the child's fear of the parents fades—as it inevitably will—the child will stray from the path that was imposed because it is incompatible with his path.

Finally, here are three verses suggesting that collaboration might be a good idea:

Let each of you look not only to his own interests, but also to the interests of others. (Philippians 2:4)

Do two walk together unless they have agreed to do so? (Amos 3:3)

If a house is divided against itself, that house cannot stand. (Mark 3:25)

Question: My parents hit me, and I turned out fine.
Answer: Good that you turned out fine. But the spanking was unnecessary and still the most toxic response.

Question: Don't you think it's important for kids to be held accountable and to take responsibility for their actions?

Answer: Too often, the phrases *hold the child accountable* and *make him take responsibility* are really codes for *punishment*. And many parents turn to punishment almost automatically when their kid isn't meeting their expectations. If the initial punishment doesn't get the job done, the parents then assume that the punishments weren't painful enough. So they add more pain, in the form of more severe punishment. Over time, they often have a lot of added pain to show for their efforts, but very little progress. When a kid is "held accountable" in this way, he isn't involved in the process at all. But if a kid is involved in the process of resolving the incompatibilities in his life and partnering with you to make things better, he's taking responsibility and being held accountable in ways that are far more meaningful.

. . . . .

Let's meet one more family.

The sun was just coming up as Kayla opened the door to her boyfriend Tony's apartment after another night at the hospital as a nurse's aide. Working nights and sleeping during the day wouldn't have been her first choice, but it was reliable money. Living with Tony wasn't necessarily her first choice either, but money was behind that decision too. She and Tony got along better when they lived separately, mostly because Tony had an old-school mentality when it came to disciplining kids, and Kayla's thirteen-year-old son, Brandon, gave him ample opportunity to point out all of Kayla's disciplinary shortcomings. Old-school mentality aside, she thought it was good for Brandon to have a male role model, and Tony did a lot of things with Brandon, taking him to baseball games, watching sports on TV together, and coaching his little league team. Still, she always tried to arrive home in time to wake Brandon up for school. If she left that up to Tony, it got ugly fast.

She took a deep breath as she entered Brandon's bedroom for The Awakening. "Brandon," she whispered as she softly rubbed his back.

"Mmpff," came the muffled response.

"Brandon, honey, you need to get up to go to school."

"Five more minutes," he mumbled. This was actually one of his more promising responses.

Five minutes later, Kayla tried again.

"Brandon, it's been five minutes. Time to get up. I don't want you to be late."

"I'm not going today," he mumbled, returning to form and rolling over.

"Brandon, come on. I've been working all night. I don't want to do this today."

"OK, then just leave me alone."

"Brandon, I want to go to sleep."

"Go to sleep. I'll get up soon."

"I'm not going to sleep until you get up." Kayla eyed the bedroom door, hoping Tony wouldn't appear.

"It's OK if I'm late," Brandon mumbled. "I have study hall first period."

"If the school thought it was OK, then they wouldn't give you a detention every time you're late. Let's go."

"I need a day off. Just one day."

"Brandon, please. I don't like working nights, but I do it because I have no choice. You don't have a choice either. Get up."

Brandon didn't budge. As she often did, Kayla briefly compared the wrath of Brandon's school and the wrath of Tony. Deciding that the two options were equally unpleasant, she yanked the sheets off Brandon's bed.

The anticipated loud swearing from Brandon prompted the appearance of Tony in Brandon's doorway. "Keep him away from me," Brandon said, suddenly swinging his feet around to get out of bed.

"Are you giving your mom a hard time about getting out of bed again?" said Tony.

"I'm out," said Brandon.

"We're managing OK here," said Kayla.

"Didn't sound OK." Tony glared at Brandon.

"He's just on his way to the shower," said Kayla, relieved to see that Brandon was now shuffling toward the door of his bedroom.

As Brandon made his way past Tony at the doorway, Tony raised his hand and feigned a smack to his head.

"Leave him be!" Kayla admonished, before realizing her words were unnecessary.

"You've been leaving him be since he was little," Tony said. "That's why he doesn't listen to you. That kid only understands one language."

Kayla started replacing the sheets on Brandon's bed. "He just has a hard time getting up in the morning." Kayla regretted her participation in a routine discussion that never went anywhere. "Smacking him around doesn't make it better."

"You let me smack him around for a week, I guarantee you he doesn't have any more trouble getting out of bed in the morning."

Kayla decided against fueling Tony's fire. If she said nothing, it would die out faster.

"Look at you, making his bed for him," Tony chided. "Like he's living in a hotel."

Kayla waited for Tony's usual next line and wasn't disappointed.

"He wouldn't have lasted five minutes growing up in my family."

Kayla finished with the bed and called to Brandon through the bathroom door. "What do you want for breakfast?"

"Like a damn hotel," grumbled Tony, shaking his head in disgust.

Chapter 4

YOUR OPTIONS

Let's start talking in much more specific terms about *your* child. Hopefully, you've been thinking about her already as you've been reading.

When your child is having no difficulty meeting your expectations, you can relax a little. She's getting along with her siblings. She's getting her homework done. Her grades are good. Her soccer coach is satisfied with her effort. Her hygiene is fine. She has friends. She seems happy. Just keep your eyes open, because incompatibility is inevitable, and the good times won't last forever.

How will you recognize that there's incompatibility? That's usually fairly straightforward: it's evident when your child is having difficulty meeting an expectation. And perhaps she's also exhibiting some challenging behaviors in response to the exhorting and extorting strategies you've deployed to get her to meet the expectation (you read about those in the last chapter).

Henceforth, we're going to think of expectations your child is having difficulty meeting as *problems that need to be solved*, and we're going to refer to them as *unsolved problems*. Our first goal is to identify those unsolved problems, and you'll probably find it helpful to make a list. The list is really important; if you don't know what expectations your child is having difficulty meeting, you won't know what to focus on when it comes to improving compatibility.

Many parents find it difficult to generate the list. Parents often find it easier to name the *behaviors* a child is exhibiting in response to unsolved problems. But the behaviors aren't the unsolved problems; they're the *by-products* of the unsolved problems. To assist, here's a small sampling of possibilities of unsolved problems:

Difficulty playing alone after school

Difficulty staying with a babysitter

Difficulty going to school

Difficulty getting to school on time

Difficulty waking up in the morning on school days

Difficulty falling asleep at night

Difficulty sleeping in her own bed at night

Difficulty getting dressed in the morning on school days

Difficulty getting ready for school in the morning

Difficulty getting ready for bed at night

Difficulty completing chores (each chore would be a separate unsolved problem)

Difficulty completing homework assignments (each assignment would be a separate unsolved problem)

Difficulty watching TV with sibling

Difficulty sharing toys with sibling

Difficulty cleaning up toys before bed

Difficulty keeping room clean

Difficulty emptying the dishwasher

Difficulty taking turns on video games with friends on playdates

Difficulty making and keeping friends

Difficulty attending birthday parties

Difficulty sitting next to sibling in the car

Difficulty sitting in the car to go grocery shopping

Difficulty sitting in car seat or wearing seat belt

Difficulty staying next to the cart at the supermarket

Difficulty coming inside from playing outside

Difficulty playing with other kids on the playground

Difficulty coming home on time for curfew

Difficulty eating healthy foods

Difficulty getting enough sleep

Difficulty completing college applications

Difficulty finding things to do besides watch TV and play video games

Difficulty turning off the TV to come to dinner

Difficulty attending soccer practice

Difficulty feeding the dog in the morning

Difficulty taking out the trash on Tuesdays

Difficulty studying for the SATs

Now, you might be thinking that in the grand scheme of things, some of the items in this list are fairly mundane. And you'd be right. Though many problems may well be mundane, how you go about solving them is absolutely crucial.

Notice a few important things about the wording of these unsolved problems:

- They all start with the word *difficulty*.
- They don't include any of the *challenging behaviors* your

child is exhibiting in response to those problems (again, those are her *behaviors*; you're interested in solving the problems that are *causing* those behaviors).

- There are *no theories* about the cause of the unsolved problem (*she just doesn't care, she enjoys pushing my buttons, she's bored, she's lazy, she's anxious, it's sibling rivalry*).
- They are *quite specific* rather than global (*Difficulty getting along with others* is global; *Difficulty agreeing with brother about what TV show to watch* is specific).

You'll see why the wording is important when it comes time to introduce the unsolved problem to your child as a prelude to solving it. We'll get to that in the next chapter.

If your child is sometimes, but not always, having difficulty meeting an expectation, it's still an unsolved problem. In other words, you're not limiting your list to expectations that are unmet *100 percent* of the time. If your child is having difficulty *reliably* meeting an expectation, it's an unsolved problem.

If my child meets the expectation sometimes, doesn't that prove she can meet it when she wants to?

No, it doesn't prove that at all. It proves that there are conditions that set the stage for your child to meet the expectation and conditions that make it much harder, and that those conditions need to be better understood.

The list can cause some parents to start feeling overwhelmed, especially if it makes clear that there are actually quite a few unsolved problems. However, the list—even if it's lengthy—should actually help you feel *less* overwhelmed, because at least now you're clear about the problems you and your child could be busy solving.

It's a lot more overwhelming to be in conflict with your child and not know what unsolved problems are causing it. If you have a long list, you may be wondering why so many problems have remained unsolved. Possibly because the way in which you've been solving these problems hasn't been working well. It's also possible that you've been more focused on *modifying behaviors* than on *solving problems*, and modifying behaviors doesn't solve the problems that are causing those behaviors.

By the way—and this is important—the biggest advantage to creating a list of unsolved problems is that it sets the stage for solving them *proactively*, rather than emergently or reactively. A lot of, if not most, parental efforts to deal with unsolved problems takes place in the heat of the moment. When it comes to solving problems durably, the heat of the moment is very poor timing.

Once you have your list, you'll want to give thought to whether your child is actually *capable* of meeting each expectation. In other words, is the expectation *realistic*? Can she really do the work in math? Can she take out the trash reliably? Can she share the remote control with her brother when they're watching TV together? Can she sit still at dinner? Can she wake up and get ready for school on time? Can she make and keep friends? Notice there's a distinction between what you *want* your child to do and what she's actually *capable* of doing. Just because you *want* her to meet an expectation doesn't mean she *can*. For many parents, those lines often are blurred.

The *kids do well if they can* and *doing well is preferable* themes are going to help out a lot here. We're going to operate on the assumption—one that's going to serve you well—that your child would *prefer* to meet expectations and that something is making it difficult for her to do so. Your energy should be devoted to getting a handle on what's making it difficult for her to meet the expectation reliably.

How do you figure that out? Perhaps your intuition will help, though parental intuition is less accurate and more imperfect than we tend to think. Perhaps a teacher or mental health or medical professional has intuition or expertise to offer on some unsolved problems, though their intuition and expertise is fallible as well. Psychoeducational testing can sometimes provide useful information about why a child is having difficulty with academics, making friends, or meeting your behavioral expectations, though testing doesn't always tell the tale. And there are other tests—related to allergies, blood sugar, and so forth—that can provide information about physiologic factors that could be affecting your child's attention span, energy level, or mood and making it difficult for her to meet certain expectations.

But your primary source of information, if you follow the guidance provided in this book, is *your child*.

Next, you're going to need some *priorities*. In other words, you need to decide which unsolved problems you want to start working on first, since it would be counterproductive to try solving them all at once. Working on too many problems at once is a good way to ensure that none get solved. If you're working on more than three unsolved problems with your child, you're probably working on too many at once. By the way, it's perfectly fine to involve your child in making decisions about which unsolved problems to prioritize.

Now, and not a moment too soon, we're ready to start considering your options for solving problems. As you'll see, we've been informally thinking about your options already.

THE PLANS

· · · · ·

I've created a simple framework outlining the three ways in which parents and other caregivers most frequently solve problems with kids. Though I've been applying the framework to behaviorally challenging kids for a very long time, it's just as applicable to the not-so-challenging variety. As you've read, behaviorally challenging kids really don't differ dramatically from not-so-behaviorally-challenging kids; they just tend to lack more skills, respond in ways that are more extreme when there's incompatibility, and often have longer lists of unsolved problems. The three options are called Plan A, Plan B, and Plan C.

Plan A refers to solving a problem *unilaterally*. Plan B involves solving a problem *collaboratively*. And Plan C involves *modifying, adapting, or setting aside* an unsolved problem, at least for now, or *holding off on helping* to see if your child can solve the problem on her own.

By the way, if a child is already meeting a given expectation, you don't need a Plan, because it's not an unsolved problem. For example, if your child is completing her homework on time and to your satisfaction, you don't need a Plan, because your expectation is being met. If your child is getting out of bed and off to school on time and without great difficulty, you don't need a Plan, because the expectation is being met. If your child is feeding the dog reliably, you don't need a Plan, because the expectation is being met. And if your child is keeping you abreast of her whereabouts in accordance with your expectations, you don't need a Plan for that either. But if your child is not completing her homework or getting out of bed or feeding the dog or keeping you abreast of her whereabouts in accordance with your expectations, you have an unsolved problem and you need a Plan.

Let's take a closer look at the three Plans.

Plan A

Plan A involves solving a problem *unilaterally*, and it's very popular. When you solve a problem using Plan A, *you* are the one deciding the solution to a given unsolved problem, and you're *imposing* that solution on your child. The words "I've decided that . . ." are a good indication that Plan A is being used to solve a problem. Here are some examples:

"Because you're having difficulty completing your math homework, I've decided that you can't go outside until you complete your math homework."

"Because you are having so much difficulty getting your teeth brushed before bed, I've decided that there will be no TV or video games at night until your teeth are brushed."

"I've decided that since you seem to be having difficulty getting up for school in the morning, I'm telling your football coach that you're too tired to play on the football team."

"Because you're having difficulty picking up your toys, I've decided to put them all into storage."

Many people think the terminology *Plan A* refers to the preferred approach to solving problems with a kid. Its popularity notwithstanding, it's actually not the preferred approach. Why not? Because while Plan A incorporates your experience, wisdom, and values, it completely cuts your kid out of the picture. It eliminates her voice, concerns, point of view, beliefs, values, preferences, personality, skills, and goals. It sends a clear message that your point of view is the only one that really matters, and that her point of view won't be heard or taken into account. It eliminates any ideas she might have about potential solutions, and makes it clear that you are the only one qualified to offer solutions. It makes her completely dependent on you to solve problems *for* her. If you send a strong and continuous message that you're not interested in hearing or taking into account your child's concerns or point of view, sooner or later she's going to start sending strong and continuous messages that she's not interested in hearing or taking into account yours. There goes your influence. And eventually she may stop trying to communicate her concerns or point of view. There goes your communication. Thus, while you certainly have wisdom, experience, and values to pass along to your kid, Play A is unlikely to be the best way to do it.

One thing is certain: Plan A is completely contrary to the collaborative partnership you're trying to establish with your child. It's also likely to bring out the worst in you and your child, especially if she's not enthusiastic about going along with your solutions. In fact, Plan A often simply begets Plan A:

Parent: If you don't make it home by curfew, I'm taking away your cellphone.

Kid: If you take away my cellphone, I'll never come home by curfew.

Even if she willingly goes along with your solutions, she's not learning how to solve the problems that affect her life.

Solutions arrived at through Plan A are not only unilateral, they're also *uninformed*. With Plan A, you're not trying to find out what's getting in the way of your kid completing her math homework, or what's making it difficult for her to brush her teeth before bed, or why she's having so much difficulty keeping you abreast of her whereabouts. You're just insisting on having your expectations met, imposing solutions, and administering adult-imposed consequences when mere insistence and your solutions don't get the job done.

As we learned from Elijah Ben Solomon in the last chapter, with many younger kids, you can get away with Plan A, mostly because you're bigger and more powerful. But you won't always be bigger, and you don't want your relationship with your child—or your influence—to be founded on something so fleeting. While power struggles are commonplace in the Dictatorial Kingdom, they're pretty much unheard of in the Collaborative Territories.

Now, a very important question: Why do the problems that affect kids' lives so often cause conflict between us and them? The answer: it traces back to how we've been trying to solve those problems. But dealing with incompatibility doesn't need to be adversarial. The problems affecting your child's life don't need to cause conflict. Parenting isn't about us versus them.

So, then, why is Plan A so popular? Use of Plan A may be driven by a variety of factors:

- worry, anxiety, and/or anger over the child not meeting a given expectation
- angst over how the child's long-term outcome will be affected if the expectation remains unmet *forever*
- comparing the child to other kids who aren't having difficulty meeting the expectation
- concern over how the child is being perceived by others
- the feeling that something decisive must be done—*right now!*—to get the child back on track
- a lack of alternative strategies for solving problems

Those are things a lot of parents feel. But those feelings don't have to lead you to Plan A. You do have other options.

At first, many adults come to the conclusion that "having an expectation" or "telling a kid what to do" are the same thing as using Plan A. This can be a major point of confusion. Having an expectation (e.g., brush your teeth before you go to bed) and voicing it is one thing; again, if that expectation is met, you don't need a Plan. If that expectation is unmet, Plan A would involve insisting harder or the threat or application of a unilateral, imposed solution (e.g., no TV until the teeth are brushed). Expectations, especially the realistic variety, are a wonderful thing. Responding to unmet expectations with Plan A, not so much.

Let's make sure that point is clear. In the following dialogues, the parent is *not* using Plan A, but rather voicing an *expectation* that the child is then *meeting*:

Kid (age 9): Mom, I want to get my ears pierced.

Mom (voicing an expectation but not using Plan A): I'd rather you not get your ears pierced until you're a little older.

Kid: How old?

Mom: I don't know—maybe thirteen.

Kid: OK.

Kid (age 17): Can I drive the car over to George's house?

Father (voicing an expectation and concern but not using Plan A): I'd rather you not. The roads are icy, and you don't have much practice driving in those conditions yet.

Kid: Oh . . . uh, so can you drive me over there, then?

Father: Sure.

Kid (age 17): I'm going to Stevie's party tonight.

Parent (voicing an expectation but not using Plan A): Um, I'm thinking you have five college applications due in two days that you haven't completed yet. I think you should stay home tonight and do your applications.

Kid: Come on—I'll only go for a few hours!

Parent: I don't think that's a smart move. You can go to a party any-time, but your collegeapplications are due in two days.

Kid: OK.

. . . . .

Now here's an example of Plan A (and its aftermath) in one of the families you've already met.

Dan knew before he opened the front door that Taylor had arrived before him. The screaming could be heard through the door.

"You are so grounded," he heard Kristin yell. (Just to be clear, this is a unilateral solution to the problem of Kristin not being aware of Taylor's whereabouts.)

"What are you gonna do? Lock me in my room?" Taylor screamed back.

Dan closed the front door. The screaming stopped. Then he heard Kristin say, "Let's just see what Dad thinks of this situation."

"Great," muttered Dan, his stomach growling. He walked toward the kitchen. Taylor intercepted him, with Kristin in tow.

"She's getting an app to lock my cell phone whenever she feels like it!" Taylor said. "All 'cuz I didn't answer it." (This is another unilateral solution to the same unsolved problem.)

"I still don't know where she was!" Kristin pled her case. "I'm not living like this!"

"Why don't you trust me?" Taylor held up her hands in frustration.

"Dan, tell her why I don't trust her," said Kristin.

"Do you guys mind if I just put my briefcase down?" Dan said, as he tried to navigate his way into the kitchen. He looked at Kristin and Taylor. "This is daily between you two. And you put me right in the middle."

"So don't be in the middle," said Kristin. "*Support* me."

"Why would he support *you*?" asked Taylor. "You're a witch."

"I'm a witch? Do witches drive their daughters to ballet? And to hip-hop? Do witches send their daughters to summer camp? Do witches buy their daughters Ariana Grande tickets? If I'm a witch, then I'm freaking Glinda."

"Who the hell is Glinda?" demanded Taylor.

"She's the Good Witch of the North," Dan tried to explain, as he scanned his options in the refrigerator. "From *The Wizard of Oz.*"

"It doesn't matter who freaking Glinda is!" yelled Kristin. Dan looked at her. For a brief moment he was sure he saw steam coming out of her ears. "What matters is that I don't know where my freaking daughter is half the time because she doesn't tell me where she's going and she won't answer her freaking cell phone!"

"I don't answer my cell phone because you call me, like, fifty times a day!" Taylor screamed back.

"Are we exaggerating for Dad's sake?"

"Barely," Taylor huffed.

"Where were you?" Dan asked.

"I was at Brooke's house, working on the physics project we're doing together."

"You and Brooke are doing a project together?" asked Kristin. "How come I didn't know that?"

"There's a lot of things going on in my life that you don't know about."

"So why didn't you answer your cell phone?"

"Because I didn't want you bugging me in the middle of working with Brooke. I blocked your calls. All you do is bug me. It's embarrassing. You think I'm a delinquent."

"You weren't at Scott's house?"

"No, I wasn't at Scott's house! Why don't you ask Brooke's mother where I was?"

Having found little of interest in the refrigerator, Dan started peeling a banana.

"I'm not calling Brooke's mother to find out if you were really there!" Kristin bellowed. "Then the rest of the world would know that I don't have the slightest freaking idea where my daughter is most of the time!"

"Why do you even care where I am most of the time? All you do is give me a hard time no matter where I am! I can't do anything right!"

Like a switch had been thrown, Kristin suddenly turned tender. "You do a lot right. I worry about you." Now Kristin was starting to tear up.

"Don't start crying!" Taylor pleaded. She looked at Dan. "I'll go back to Brooke's if she starts crying."

Dan stopped chewing. "I think maybe you two should give it a rest for the night."

"Is she shutting down my cell phone?" asked Taylor.

"I think we should deal with the cell phone problem later," said Dan.

"She better not shut down my cell phone," Taylor warned, as she stalked off to her room.

If that sounded familiar, well, perhaps that's because Plan A is very popular. Our goal is to dramatically reduce your reliance on Plan A for handling unsolved problems.

Does reducing your reliance on Plan A mean you're dropping all the expectations you have for your child? No. You still have lots of expectations, and she's probably meeting most of them. Plan A simply isn't the ideal option for dealing with the expectations she's having *difficulty* meeting.

Does reducing your reliance on Plan A mean that you're just going to stand passively by and hope for the best if your child is having difficulty meeting expectations? No. You have more influence than that. *Parent-*

ing is not a constant balancing act between conflict and capitulation.

Is Plan A out of your repertoire completely? No, it's still an option under some (especially emergent) conditions, just not one you want to turn to very often.

Plan B

Plan B involves solving a problem *collaboratively*. Fair warning: the conventional wisdom—and many popular parenting books and TV personalities—would advise you against collaborating with your child. After all, you're in charge. But in this book, being "in charge" means that (1) you recognize that if your child is having difficulty meeting specific expectations, something must be getting in her way; (2) you also recognize that you're on the hook for figuring out what's getting in the way, and that your child is likely to be your best source of information; and (3) you're skilled at working together with your child to help her solve problems.

Plan B consists of three ingredients: the *Empathy step*, the *Define-Adult-Concerns step*, and the *Invitation step*.

1. The Empathy step involves gathering information from your child to understand her concern, perspective, or point of view on a given unsolved problem.
2. The Define-Adult-Concerns step involves communicating your concern, perspective, or point of view on the same problem.
3. The Invitation step is when you and your child discuss and agree on a solution that (a) is *realistic*, meaning both parties can actually do what they're agreeing to do, and (b) will address the concerns of *both* parties.

You'll be reading much more about these steps (with lots of examples) in the ensuing chapters.

On first hearing about Plan B, many people come to the erroneous conclusion that the best time to use Plan B is just as they are in the midst of dealing with an unsolved problem. That's Emergency Plan B, and it's actually not the best timing for solving problems. Few of us do our clearest thinking in the heat of the moment. Because you've already made a list of unsolved problems, those problems are now *highly predictable*. Because you've also decided which unsolved problems are your priorities, there's no reason to wait until the problems pop up again before you try to solve them. Problems don't pop up—it just feels that way (before you've made your list and established your priorities). The goal is to solve problems before you're in the thick of them. That's Proactive Plan B.

For example, in the case of the unsolved problem of difficulty feeding the dog, the best time to have a Plan B discussion with your child is *before* she's faced with the task of feeding the dog rather than in the heat of the moment when you're in a rush to get everyone off to school. If the unsolved problem is difficulty completing math homework, the time to have a Plan B discussion is *before* your child is struggling with her math homework.

Some parents find it helpful to make an appointment with their kids for these problem-solving discussions, and to provide advance notice of the unsolved problem that will be discussed. Some parents and kids find it useful to have a standing time each day or week at which the problem-solving discussions take place. Doing so ensures that the discussions are a reliable aspect of family life; otherwise, there's the risk that the discussions won't happen at all.

Plan B accomplishes many missions. The Empathy step helps

you gather information about what's making it difficult for your child to meet a given expectation and will also help you learn a lot about her skills, beliefs, values, preferences, personality traits, goals, and direction. The Empathy step ensures that your child's voice will be heard. The Define-Adult-Concerns step ensures that your child benefits from your experience, wisdom, and values. So your voice will be heard, too. And the Invitation step helps you and your child work toward solutions to the problems that are affecting her life in ways that address your and her concerns. It's win-win. And as you'll read in chapter 9, it's a lot more than that.

The most common complaint I hear from kids about their parents is, *"They don't listen to me."* The most common complaint I hear from parents about their kids is, *"He won't talk to me."* Those complaints are seldom heard when parents and kids are solving problems using Plan B.

Plan C

Plan C involves modifying, adapting, or setting aside an unsolved problem completely, at least temporarily. It can also involve holding off on helping to see if your child can solve a given problem independently.

Many parents read the "setting aside" part and immediately conclude that Plan C is the equivalent of "giving in." Actually, "giving in" is what happens when you attempt to solve a problem with Plan A and end up capitulating because your kid responded badly to your imposition of a solution. But the C of Plan C doesn't stand for *capitulating* or *caving.*

That's good, because many parents feel that the worst possible thing they could ever do as parents is capitulate to their child's wishes. So, at all costs, they are on guard against caving. But the fear of caving is prevalent exclusively in the Dictatorial Kingdom. You're trying to make the move to the Collaborative Territories, where deferring to your child's voice, concerns, point of view, beliefs, values, preferences, personality, skills, and goals could actually make good sense under some circumstances (in which case you wouldn't be caving at all). Plan C is a big part of being responsive to the hand you've been dealt and improving compatibility. It's intentional and thoughtful.

You might use Plan C for any of several reasons:

You don't really care that much about the expectation.

Many parents pull out all the stops on pursuing a given expectation and then, when they allow themselves the luxury of reflection, conclude that they didn't really care that much about the expectation in the first place. If you don't care that much about the expectation, set it aside.

Kid (age 11): I don't want to play soccer anymore. I'm not enjoying it, and I'm too busy anyway.

Parent: Yes, you're definitely busy. But I hate to see you give it up. You're very good, and you've been playing with Coach Brown for a long time.

Kid: I know. But I want to concentrate on lacrosse and football. And I can't do everything.

Parent (thinking): He's so good in soccer . . . but he probably does need to start concentrating on one or two sports . . . and he's been saying soccer is boring for a while now . . .

Parent (speaking): That's a good point. OK, I'm fine with you dropping soccer. We'll need to think of a good way to let Coach Brown know.

In lieu of your experience, wisdom, and values, you've made the conscious decision to defer to your child's skills, beliefs, values, preferences, personality traits, and goals.

You do care, but you've decided that this is an expectation on which you won't be intervening right now, because you're deferring to her beliefs, values, preferences, traits, goals, and direction. Set it aside, at least for now (Plan C).

Kid (age 15): Mom, I'm going to get my hair cut in a Mohawk.

Parent: Huh?

Kid: I want to get my hair cut in a Mohawk.

Parent: But you have such beautiful hair.

Kid: Yeah, but Mohawks are cool. And some of the other guys on the football team are doing it.

Parent (thinking): He is going to look so stupid in a Mohawk . . . but I guess it's a team thing . . . at least it's not an earring . . .

Parent (speaking): OK.

You've decided to give your child the opportunity to solve the problem independently.

You do care, but your child has requested that you remain uninvolved in solving the problem or you want to give her the opportunity to solve it on her own.

Parent: I received an e-mail from your history teacher telling me that you've fallen behind on some assignments.

Kid (age 16): I can't believe she e-mailed you!

Parent: Well, I think she just wants to keep me informed.

Kid: Did you e-mail back?

Parent: No, not yet. I wanted to talk to you about it first.

Kid: Good!

Parent: Have you fallen behind on some of your assignments?

Kid: A little. I took on too much this semester. I'll get caught up. But I don't want you to get involved. I can deal with this on my own.

Parent: OK. I'm not feeling like I need to get involved. Are you going to meet with her to talk about it?

Kid: Yes—I just haven't gotten to it yet.

Parent: OK. Keep me posted. I do feel like I should e-mail her back. I'll just let her know that you and I have talked about it and that you'll take it from there.

The expectation is unrealistic for your child at this point in her development.

You do care, but you've concluded that your child isn't able to reliably meet the expectation at this point. Wishful thinking won't serve you well. Set it aside, at least for now (Plan C).

Parent: Jimmy invited you to do a sleepover on Saturday night. Do you want to go?

Kid (age 8): No. I don't want to do a sleepover. I never did a sleepover before.

Parent: I know. I was thinking we could try it. What do you think?

Kid: I think I would be scared sleeping in his house. And I'm afraid of what will happen if I have an accident.

Parent: Oh, you mean you're worried that you'll wet the bed?

Kid: Yeah.

Parent (thinking): That would be very embarrassing for him . . . and I don't know how well Jimmy's parents would handle it . . .

Parent (speaking): Hmm. I understand. Should I tell his mom that you'd love to come over that day but not for a sleepover?

Kid: Yeah. But don't tell her about the accident part.
Parent: OK.

You have other higher-priority expectations to pursue.

If you've concluded that your child can reliably meet the expectation but you've decided to prioritize other expectations, drop it,
at least for now (Plan C). Remember, if you try to solve too many
problems at once, you'll reduce your odds of solving any at all.

*Parent: Alicia, you know how there are a few problems we've decided to
start working on? We're working on helping you and your sister figure out
who's going to sit in the front seat when we're in the car . . . and we're working on helping you not be on your cell phone so late at night that you don't
get enough sleep . . . and we're working on how you and your brother have
been having difficulty watching TV together. I'm thinking that's plenty of
problems to be working on right now. How 'bout we hold off on working
on the difficulty you've been having eating dinner with the family for now?
We'll work on that after we get some of those other problems solved.*

Alicia: So I don't have to eat dinner with the family?

Parent: Not for now . . . not while we're working on those other problems.

Some parents have great difficulty temporarily deferring expectations. Often this is because they feel that every expectation is of
extreme importance. Every expectation can't be of extreme importance. *If everything is equally important, then nothing is important.*

. . . . . .

Here's another example of Plan C:

Denise was in the basement doing some organizing and came across a
box with mementos from the kids' early years. The box was filled with old

T-shirts the kids had worn, small toys they had played with, even old report cards. She started looking at Nick's early report cards and found herself reflecting on his early school years, the ones where she first discovered that academics were not going to be smooth sailing for him. She remembered one night in particular, almost as if it had happened yesterday. Her mother was at the house visiting:

Nick had been in the second grade, sitting at the kitchen table trying to complete a writing assignment for homework.

"I don't know how to do this!" he had said, after struggling to write for over an hour.

Denise remembered that, back then, she felt it was very important for Nick to learn the value of persistence and hard work. "Stick with it, buddy—you'll get it," she said.

"I don't know what to write!" Nick said.

"Well, I could tell you what to write, but then it would be my words and not yours," Denise replied.

Nick suddenly became teary-eyed. "I don't know what words to use."

Denise looked at the description of the assignment. "You're supposed to write two paragraphs on something you like to do for fun. Come on—you can do that. Think about things you like to do. There are lots of things you like to do."

"I don't know what words to use!" Nick insisted, his voice rising.

This wasn't the first time Nick had said this, but it was the first time his words resonated with Denise. She saw that the sheet of paper in front of Nick was still completely blank.

"What do you mean, you don't know what words to use?"

"I can't think of the words," Nick said.

"Do you know what you want to write about?" asked Denise.

"Drawing," said Nick.

"OK, so write about drawing. What do you like about drawing?"

"It's fun . . . and there's nobody screaming at you to try harder," said Nick.

"OK, so write that."

"I don't know how to start. And I don't know how to spell *drawing*."

"*Drawing* is d-r-a-w-i-n-g. What do you mean, you don't know how to start?"

"I need you to start it for me," said Nick.

"You mean the first sentence?" said Denise, a bit baffled.

"Yes!" said Nick, relieved that he'd finally made himself clear.

"You mean, like, 'One of my favorite activities is drawing,'" suggested Denise.

Nick immediately began furiously writing the sentence. "What should I write after that?"

"You should say what you like about drawing," said Denise.

"I need the words," pleaded Nick.

"Um, how about 'Here are some of the things I like about drawing,'" Denise volunteered.

Nick again quickly wrote the sentence.

Denise's mother had been observing the scene from the kitchen sink and could no longer resist weighing in. "Are you going to write the whole thing for him?" she asked.

"He's been struggling with it for an hour, and I really don't see the point in prolonging this. Sitting there writing nothing isn't helping him."

"You gonna go to college with him? Write everything for him there too?" the grandmother asked.

"He's not in college, Mom. He's in the second grade. It's not like he doesn't *want* to do it. It's like he . . . *can't*."

"What do you mean, he can't? Of course he can!"

"We go through this every time he has a writing assignment," Denise reflected. "I'm starting to think maybe something's not right."

"If something wasn't right, don't you think they would've caught it at school?"

"How do I know? But I'm calling his teacher tomorrow. I wonder if she knows how much time we spend on homework every night."

Denise suddenly noticed that Nick was now writing a few sentences on his own. "You doing OK now, buddy?" she asked.

"Yeah. I just needed help getting started," said Nick.

Does Denise plan on perpetually setting aside the expectation that Nick independently get started on writing assignments? No. When will that become an expectation again? When she thinks it's realistic.

And once again, what if you've decided that you *do* care about the unsolved problem, it *is* realistic, it *is* a high priority, and you're *not* OK letting your child go it alone on solving it? Solve the problem collaboratively, using Plan B. How do you do that? Well, you now know the three steps, but you'll be getting the nuts and bolts in the next chapter.

Q & A

Question: What if I'm really determined to get a problem solved? Plan A, right?

Answer: Just because you're determined to solve a problem doesn't mean Plan A is the best way to solve it. Your determination will serve you well when you're using Plan B too.

Question: But isn't it my role as a parent to be *decisive*?

Answer: Not if you're limiting your definition of "decisiveness" to *imposing solutions*. Your decisiveness will serve you well if it helps you come to the recognition that there's a problem that needs to be solved.

Question: Why not start with Plan A and then move over to Plan B if Plan A doesn't work?
Answer: The question implies that Plan A is preferable and should be the instinctive approach to solving problems. Plan B is actually preferable and should be the instinctive approach to solving problems.

Question: So I'm not losing any authority when I'm using Plan B?
Answer: None whatsoever. And in the meantime, you're picking up a partner.

Question: My friends tell me I'm a helicopter parent. They say I'm always micromanaging my kids. I just want things to go well for them. That's not good?
Answer: It's great that you want things to go well for your kids. And your involvement in your kids' lives is admirable. But you're not going to be around forever, so it's just as important for you to set the stage for them to solve life's problems and set a course without you. And it's important for them to begin thinking independently of you, because you're not them and they're not you.

Question: I'm a sink-or-swim guy. Not good?
Answer: If your kid already knows how to swim through all

the choppy waters she's facing in life, you're all set. But since there are some big waves she's having difficulty surmounting, she's going to need you to broaden your parenting perspective and repertoire.

Question: Isn't it good for kids to fear their parents a little?
Answer: Lots of kids stay on the straight and narrow because of fear, at least initially. But fear is fleeting. Once the fear is gone—and sooner or later, it *should* be gone—they lose their bearings because they never had the opportunity to think about and explore their own values, preferences, and beliefs. It was just fear governing their behavior. Again, you want them looking *inside* to get their bearings.

Question: Is it just parental expectations that could cause incompatibility, or could a kid also be having difficulty meeting her own expectations?
Answer: Parents are usually the ones setting expectations, at least early on. But it's certainly true that many kids start to have expectations for themselves—for example, who they want to be friends with, what scores they expect to receive on a test, and so forth—and if they're having difficulty meeting those expectations, there's still incompatibility and there are still problems to be solved.

· · · · ·

Kayla was putting Brandon's laundered clothes into his dresser before he came home from school. As she placed one of his T-shirts in a drawer, she noticed a folded piece of paper. It was his semester report from school.

She knew semester grades were coming out soon but hadn't realized they'd already been released. As she looked at his grades, it slowly dawned on her that Brandon might have been intentionally hiding the report card. The failing grade in history was the dead giveaway, though his grades in other classes weren't great either. Kayla sat down on Brandon's bed and read the comments from his history teacher:

Brandon performed poorly on our two major tests this semester— his average score was a 47. He's been less active in our class discussions as well. Brandon needs to be more diligent in studying for tests and needs to come to class prepared to discuss the material. I look forward to seeing greater effort in the coming semester.

"Oh my," Kayla said out loud, a bit stunned. Brandon had never failed a class before. And his effort had never been questioned. Her shock quickly turned to anger. "He's *hiding* his report card? Like I'm not going to find out that he failed his history class? Unbelievable." She refolded the report card, placed it in her pocket, and awaited Brandon's arrival from school, pondering whether it was the grade or the hiding that was more irksome and contemplating her punishment options.

Brandon arrived home fifteen minutes later and sensed that something was amiss. "What's the matter?" he asked.

Kayla pulled the report card out of her pocket and held it up. "This."

"You found it."

"Were you hiding it?"

"I was going to show it to you."

"When? After you fail history again?"

"No . . ."

"Then when?"

"I don't know . . ."

"Well, I've seen it now."

Brandon said nothing.

"You want to tell me how you managed to fail history?" she asked.

"I don't know."

"You want to tell me why I didn't know you were failing history?"

"I didn't want you to be mad."

"Well, I'm mad now."

"And I didn't want Tony to know."

This gave Kayla brief pause. "Has he been helping you with your homework?"

"I don't want his help."

"You're failing history and you don't want his help?"

"He just yells at me. That's not help."

"How come you didn't tell me?"

Brandon shrugged.

"Brandon, how come you didn't tell me?"

"Tell you what?"

"That Tony hasn't been helping you with your homework."

Brandon shrugged again.

"Don't you think that's something I'd want to know?"

"I didn't want to start a fight."

"Well, I can't help you with your homework. I'm usually at work when you're supposed to be doing your homework."

"I know."

The two stared at each other.

"Can I go to my room?" Brandon asked.

"What are we doing about this report card?"

"I don't know."

At work that night, Kayla found herself preoccupied with Brandon's report card.

"You're quiet tonight," said one of the other nurse's aides, Cheryl, as they sat in the nurse's station.

"I guess I have a lot on my mind."

"You worried about Mr. Beason?" Cheryl asked, referring to the patient who'd just been moved to their floor from intensive care. "I can take care of him if you want."

"No, no, I can handle Mr. Beason. I'm not worried about him."

"Oh. Well, I don't mean to pry." Cheryl turned back to her computer screen.

"Just some trouble with my son. And I can't do anything about it because I'm here."

"What kind of trouble?"

"He's failing history, and he hid his report card from me."

Cheryl's knowing look didn't make Kayla feel any better. "Ah, the hidden report card. I had a few of those."

Kayla recalled that Cheryl's kids were older. "You did?"

"Of course. What kid doesn't hide his report card from his parents?"

"My kid never did," said Kayla. "Until today."

"Did you ask him about it?"

"Well, now that I think of it, it was more of an interrogation."

Cheryl laughed. "You were upset."

"Hell yes, I was upset. I want him to do better than me. I moved in with my boyfriend so Brandon could go to a better school. Now he's failing history and hiding his report cards?"

"Hmm. What did he say about why he's failing history?"

"He didn't say much. But I don't think I gave him much of a chance."

"Well, that's the thing about interrogations." Cheryl smiled.

"Except that he doesn't want my boyfriend helping him with his homework. Says all he does is yell at him."

"Doesn't sound like the ideal homework situation," Cheryl observed.

"Yeah, well it's not like we have much choice," said Kayla. "I'm here most nights. That's when the homework gets done. So I don't know what to do."

"What does Brandon say about what you should do?"

"How's he going to know what to do? I'm the parent."

"Yeah, but that doesn't make you a genius . . . or a mind reader. One of the things I had to learn the hard way with my kids—and it took me a long time to learn it—is that I didn't have to solve all their problems for them. And that they had a much better idea of what was getting in their way than I did."

"I don't follow you."

"All you know is that Brandon failed history and doesn't want your boyfriend's help. But you don't really know why he's failing history. So how could you know what to do about it?"

"What do you mean, I don't know why he's failing history? His teacher said he's just not putting forth the effort."

Cheryl laughed again. "Teachers always say that! You might want to ask Brandon."

"I was just going to ground him until he starts getting better grades in history."

"How would that fix whatever's causing him to be failing history?"

Kayla pondered this question. "Well, he needs to know that the history grade needs to come up."

"I bet he wants his history grade to come up too!"

Kayla considered this as well. "But don't you think he needs my help?"

"Maybe. But I don't know if it's the kind of help you're thinking of giving him."

The patient in room 1212 was now pushing her call button. "Mrs. Cohen. She's yours," said Cheryl. "You want me to go?"

"No, I'll go," said Kayla. "Her problems are usually pretty easy to solve. It'll be a nice change of pace for me."

Under duress most human beings head for Plan A. But since unsolved problems are predictable—after all, you now have your list and your priorities—you can solve them proactively and therefore won't find yourself in a state of duress as often. Second, if you and your child have a collaborative partnership, you aren't on the hook for solving all of her problems; you're doing it together. Third, the unsolved problems you have on your list are likely to remain unsolved so long as you don't have the information you need from your partner.

Chapter 5

SOLVING PROBLEMS TOGETHER

Why do adults have such a hard time solving problems collaboratively with kids? In the first place, it often seems a whole lot easier and more efficient to simply insist on what you want your kid to do. But now you know: simply insisting on what you want and demanding compliance isn't the ideal approach. Not if you want to partner with him in solving them. And not if you want to foster the more positive characteristics of human nature in your child. Plus, eventually—and ideally—he's going to stop responding well to your insisting anyway.

But there's another reason solving problems collaboratively is hard: many adults haven't had much practice at it, having been raised by parents who were probably highly skilled at demanding and insisting. So we'll have to get you some practice. Your child is going to need some practice too. After all, you're in this together.

As you read in the last chapter, there are three steps involved in solving a problem collaboratively: the Empathy step, the Define-Adult-Concerns step, and the Invitation step. Let's take a much closer look at each. This, by the way, is the most technical chapter in the book; you may feel the need to read it more than once.

THE EMPATHY STEP:
CHILDREN ARE TO BE HEARD
(AND UNDERSTOOD)

Here's what you know about the Empathy step already: it's where you'll be gathering information about your child's concern, perspective, or point of view on a specific expectation he's having difficulty meeting. You also know that you'll be doing that proactively as often as possible.

Just like adults, kids have important, valid concerns: hunger, fatigue, fear, the desire to buy or do certain things, and the tendency to avoid things that are scary or that make them uncomfortable or at which they don't feel competent. Your mission in the Empathy step is to demonstrate to your child that you're really interested in and curious about those concerns.

You're not teaching any lessons in the Empathy step. Actually, you're not teaching lessons in *any* of the three steps. You're not being judgmental either. You're also not saying many of the standard things adults say in response to kids' concerns. So you wouldn't respond to "I'm afraid there's a monster under my bed" with "Oh, come on, there's no monster under your bed." You wouldn't respond to "The label in my shirt is bugging me" with "Every shirt has labels, so I guess you'll have to live with it." And "I guess you'll have to man up" wouldn't be the ideal response to "The kids on the school bus are being mean." When you respond in these ways, that whooshing sound you hear is your child's concerns being ignored, disregarded, dismissed, diminished, and blown off the table.

Some adults have never considered it especially important to gather information about and understand a kid's concern, perspective, or

82

point of view. That's why many kids—perhaps most, unfortunately—are accustomed to having their concerns ignored, disregarded, dismissed, or diminished by adults. After all, we adults often think we *already know* what's getting in the kid's way on a given problem, which explains why we often don't put much energy into finding out. We have concerns of our own, which we're eager to express, and we often do it by overriding or diminishing kids' concerns. And we've already formulated incredible solutions (no need to explore, discuss, or collaborate on solutions when we've already decided on one).

The bad news is that, quite often, our assumptions about kids' concerns are way off base. That's why our incredible solutions often turn out to be less than incredible. Still more bad news: kids who are accustomed to having their concerns dismissed tend to be far less receptive to hearing the concerns of their caregivers. Plus, as you've read, if you're not interested in your child's concerns and if you're not trying hard to ensure that those concerns are heard, clarified, and addressed, eventually your child will stop talking to you. Then you won't have a problem-solving partner, the problems won't get solved, and you won't have much influence.

The good news is that your concerns *will* still be heard (in the Define-Adult-Concerns step) *and* addressed (in the Invitation step), and you'll still have a chance to offer potential solutions (also in the Invitation). More good news: you don't lose any authority by gathering information, understanding, and empathizing with your child's concerns. None. So the pressure's off: there's no need to divine your child's concern or perspective. You don't need to be a mind reader. But you do need to become highly skilled at gathering information from your child.

So how do you do it? When you're using Proactive Plan B, the information-gathering and understanding process begins with an introduction to the unsolved problem. The introduction usually begins with the words "I've noticed that . . ." and ends with the words "What's up?" In between you're inserting an unsolved problem. The introduction is made much easier if you stick with the general guidelines for writing unsolved problems you read about in chapter 4. Here are some examples:

"I've noticed that it's been difficult for you to eat breakfast before school. What's up?"

"I've noticed that it's been difficult for you to get along with your sister lately. What's up?"

"I've noticed that it's been difficult for you to feed the dog in the morning. What's up?"

"I've noticed that you haven't been too enthusiastic about riding the school bus lately. What's up?"

"I've noticed that it's been difficult for you to complete your math homework at night. What's up?"

"I've noticed that it's been difficult for you to answer your cell phone when I call you. What's up?"

"I've noticed that it's been hard for you to let us know who you're with and where you're at. What's up?"

"I've noticed you've been having difficulty getting up to go to school lately. What's up?"

Notice that, in accordance with the guidelines, these introductions do not make mention of challenging behaviors (e.g., screaming, swearing, ear flicking), do not include adult theories (e.g., "because you hate me"), and are specific rather than global. The guidelines decrease the likelihood that your child will think he's in trouble, decrease his level of defensiveness, and increase the likelihood that he'll actually respond to your inquiry. Since the main mission of the Empathy step is to gather information so as to understand your child's concern or perspective about a given problem, you badly want him to respond. If he doesn't respond, his concerns won't be identified and addressed and the problem will remain unsolved.

I should mention that the introduction is the easy part of the Empathy step. The hard part comes next. After you ask, "What's up?" one of five things is going to happen:

Possibility #1: He says something.

Possibility #2: He says nothing or "I don't know."

Possibility #3: He says, "I don't have a problem with that."

Possibility #4: He says, "I don't want to talk about it right now."

Possibility #5: He becomes defensive and says something like, "I don't have to talk to you" (or worse).

Let's flesh out each of these possibilities.

Possibility #1: He says something.

If, after the problem is introduced, your child starts talking, that's good. Now you need to keep him talking, because his initial response is unlikely to provide a clear understanding of his concern, perspective, or point of view. You're going to need to probe for more information. The probing process—which I call "drilling for information"—is pretty hard for many people, especially in the beginning, mostly because they're not sure what to say. Difficulty with drilling causes many Plan B ships to run aground, thereby causing many adults to abandon ship. The good news is that there are some strategies to help you master the drilling process so the Plan B boat stays afloat.

First, notice the word is *drill*, not *grill*. The primary goal of drilling is to *clarify*, whereas grilling tends to be an act of intimidation, or a sign that you anticipate that your child won't be forthcoming or will lie. Your goal is to demonstrate to your child that your attempt to understand his concern or perspective isn't fake or perfunctory. You're really curious . . . *you really want to understand*.

Second, *drilling* is not the same thing as *talking*. There are parents who frequently talk to (or perhaps mostly *at*) their kid but never achieve a clear understanding of their kid's concern or perspective on a specific unsolved problem. Drilling is much harder than simply talking.

Third, drilling involves *listening*, not *lessoning* (as in teaching your child a lesson) or *lessening* (as in dismissing or diminishing his concerns).

The following drilling strategies should help; they're all very effective at helping your kid feel heard, understood, and validated and at keeping him talking:

Strategy #1—use reflective listening: This is where you're simply mirroring or repeating back whatever your child just said to you. If, in response to your inquiry about not getting along well with his sister, he responds, "Because I don't like her," your response would be, "Ah, you don't like her." Then you'd add a clarifying statement, such as "How so?" or "I don't quite understand" or "I'm confused" or "Can you say more about that?" or "What do you mean?" Sound a little sappy? I thought so too thirty-five years ago when, as one of my first experiences in the field of psychology, I was trained to be a telephone hotline crisis counselor, and the primary strategy I was instructed to use was reflective listening. I've been using it ever since. I quickly learned that reflective listening is a good way to show that you're listening and that you understand. It's an effective, authentic way to keep your kid talking and to gather additional information. Reflective listening is your default strategy. If you're in the midst of the Empathy step and you're not sure what to say, reflective listening is always a safe bet.

Strategy #2—ask "W questions" (who or what or where/ when): These questions are also a good way to demonstrate that you're really listening and need additional information. Examples: "Who's been giving you a hard time on the school bus?" "What's making it hard for you to answer your cell phone?" "Where/when is your sister annoying you?" Remember, drilling is about gathering information, and "W questions" are a straightforward way to do so. Notice also that there's another "W question"—*why*—that you shouldn't be asking very often; in general, that question is going to elicit a theory, and quite possibly one that the child acquired from an adult. A long time ago—when I was still occasionally asking kids why—I asked a four-year-old girl why she was misbehaving at home. She responded, "I do it for negative reinforcement." I've been sticking with the other "W questions" ever since.

Often we adults already have the next question ready before

our kid is through answering the first one. Or we have a pre-ordained solution ready that we're just dying to propose (or impose). Those are good ways to communicate that you're not really listening or understanding.

Strategy #3—ask about the situational variability of the unsolved problem: At times, it may appear as though your child actually is capable of meeting a given expectation because he sometimes does. This often leads adults to jump to the conclusion that the child can meet the expectation *when he feels like it* and that he doesn't meet the expectation when he *doesn't* feel like it. The reality is that there may be nuanced, subtle differences between similar expectations that explain the inconsistency. Rather than jump to conclusions related to poor motivation—"I know he can do the math when we wants to! He did it yesterday!"—you'd be better off seeking clarification from your child. Remember, when you're drilling, you're off the hook for mind reading: "So, help me understand how you were able to do the math homework yesterday and you're not able to do the math homework today." "So, sometimes you get up for school pretty easily, and other times it's a lot harder. Help me understand that."

Strategy #4—ask the child what he's thinking in the midst of the unsolved problem: This is another good way to gather information about your child's concern, perspective, or point of view on a given unsolved problem. "So, when you're sitting at your desk trying to do your math homework, what are you thinking?" Notice you're not asking him what he's *feeling*. It's not that asking your child what he's feeling is a crime; it's just that the answer (happy, sad, frustrated, embarrassed, bored) doesn't generally provide you with the information you're seeking about his concern or perspective. Notice also that you're not asking him what he *needs*—that question is more likely to prompt him to offer a solution rather than a concern, and you're not ready to start thinking about solutions until the Invitation step.

Strategy #5—break the unsolved problem down into its component parts: Most unsolved problems have multiple components. For example, getting ready for bed at night has different components (taking a shower, brushing teeth, putting on pajamas, reading a book, etc.). And getting ready for school in the morning has components (waking up on time, getting out of bed, brushing teeth, taking a shower, choosing clothes, getting the backpack ready, eating breakfast, etc.). But kids sometimes need help identifying those components so they can pinpoint which component is causing them to struggle:

Parent (introduction): I've noticed it's been difficult for you to decide what clothes to wear to school in the morning. What's up?

Child: I don't know.

Parent: Do you want to think about it a little?

Child (after thinking): I really don't know.

Parent: Would it help if we thought about what's involved in deciding what clothes you're going to wear?

Child: OK.

Parent: Well, one of the things I think you do is decide whether the clothes you're going to wear make sense based on the weather that day. Is that hard?

Child: No.

Parent: So you're not having any difficulty thinking about the weather outside and deciding what to wear?

Child: No.

Parent: OK. Another thing you do is decide whether you like the way the clothes look. Is that part hard?

Child: No.

Parent: So you don't have any trouble deciding how the clothes are going to look?

Child: No.

Parent: OK—good to know. Next, you decide how the clothes are going to feel on your body. Is that hard?

Child: Yes!

Parent: Deciding how they're going to feel on your body is hard?

Child: Yes!

Parent: What's hard about that?

Child: A lot of my clothes are itchy and have labels in them and they're too tight and the labels bug me. So I can't find anything to wear.

Good to know.

Strategy #6—make a discrepant observation: This involves making an observation that differs from what the child has described about a particular situation. It's the riskiest, in terms of causing the child to stop talking, of all the drilling strategies. That's because many kids—perhaps especially those frequently accused of lying—misinterpret a discrepant observation as an accusation of dishonesty. Fortunately, you're not accusing him of lying; you're simply pointing out that your observations differ from his. Just because your experience of reality differs from your child's doesn't mean he's lying. Example: "I know you're saying that you and Charlotte are getting along fine these days, but yesterday at breakfast you two weren't getting along very well at all. What do you think was going on with that?"

Strategy #7—table (and ask for more concerns): This is where you're "shelving" some concerns the child has already articulated so as to facilitate the consideration of other concerns. You're not dismissing the earlier concerns; you're just putting them on the back burner temporarily so as to clear space for consideration of other possible concerns. Example: "So if I made pancakes every morning for breakfast, and if the pancakes were ready ten minutes before you had to leave for school, and if your brother and sister weren't annoying you, would there be anything else that would make it difficult for you to eat breakfast before leaving for school in the morning?"

Strategy #8—summarize (and ask for more concerns): This is where you're summarizing concerns you've already heard about and then asking if there are any other concerns that haven't yet been discussed. This is the recommended strategy to use before moving on to the Define-Adult-Concerns step, just to make sure there are no other concerns. Example: "Let me make sure I understand everything you've said. It's hard for you to do your social studies work sheet for homework because you're really tired after a long day at school and soccer practice, it's too noisy in the dining room because your brother is watching TV in the living room, and you need my help and sometimes I'm busy putting your sister to bed. Is there anything else that's hard for you about completing the social studies work sheet for homework?"

Here's an example of what information gathering might sound like, with examples of some of the different drilling strategies:

Parent: I've noticed that you're having difficulty sticking with our thirty-minute time limit on electronics lately. What's up?

Max: It's not fair.

Parent (using strategies 1 and 2): It's not fair. What's not fair?

Max: Thirty minutes isn't enough time.

Parent (using strategy 1): Thirty minutes isn't enough time. How so?

Max: 'Cuz you think everything counts as electronics.

Parent (using strategy 1): I think everything counts as electronics.

Max: You think Minecraft counts as electronics. And I agree with that. And you think playing Clash of Clans on my iPhone counts. And I agree with that too. But you also think texting counts. And you think Instagram counts. And you think Snapchat counts. If all that stuff is going to count, then thirty minutes isn't enough. So it's not fair.

Parent (using strategy 1): So you feel that it's not fair for me to count all of those things as electronics.

Max: Yeah! I mean, I'm not even doing that much gaming! The thirty-minute time limit was supposed to be just for gaming. But now you're counting everything with a screen as part of the thirty minutes!

Parent (using strategy 1): And you feel that things that aren't gaming shouldn't count.

Max: No! I mean, those other things are how kids communicate these days. That's how I communicate with my friends. So if those things count as electronics time, then I wouldn't have any time left for gaming.

Parent (using strategy 4): I get it. So when I'm telling you to get off your cell phone or the computer, what are you thinking?

Max: I'm thinking you're the only parent I know who thinks that other stuff counts as screen time. And I'm thinking it's not fair. And I'm thinking I wish you knew more about how kids communicate these days.

Parent (strategy 8): So you feel that it's not fair that there's a thirty-minute limit on electronics; and you feel that the stuff you're doing on a screen besides gaming shouldn't count as part of the thirty minutes; and you feel that most other parents don't think that stuff should count as screen time. Is there anything else I should know about what's getting in the way of you sticking with the thirty-minute limit on screen time?

Max: Well, you kind of freak out when you see my phone next to me when I'm doing my homework. I can text my friends while I'm doing my homework and still get my homework done. Sometimes I'm texting them about the homework.

Parent (strategy 6, the risky one): OK. Although you have told me that the texting sometimes distracts you when you're doing your homework.

Max: Yeah, sometimes, but not most of the time. Plus, if it's distracting me, I just don't pay attention to it until my homework's done.

That was pretty informative. We went all the way from "It's not fair" to a much clearer understanding of the kid's point of view on the problem that we're trying to solve. All that information is going to come in handy when we're ready to start considering solutions in the Invitation. Adults are often amazed at what they learn when they start inquiring about a kid's concerns.

Just in case you're curious, here's how it would have sounded if the parent had used Plan A to "solve" this problem:

Parent: Because you're not sticking with the thirty-minute time limit on electronics, I've decided to take away your cell phone and remove the Xbox until I decide you're ready to use them again.

And of course, if—for any of the reasons described in chapter 4—the unsolved problem is being handled with Plan C for now, you wouldn't raise the issue in the first place.

Some adults, having made some headway toward understanding their kids' concerns in the Empathy step, have difficulty resisting the temptation to revert to form by being dismissive or jumping back to unilateral solutions, thereby aborting the collaborative process. Here are some examples of what *not* to do:

Parent: I've noticed that it's been difficult for you to eat breakfast before school. What's up?

Kid: I don't like eggs.

Parent: Well, that's what's on the menu! I'm not a short-order cook.

Parent: I've noticed that it's been difficult for you to feed the dog in the morning. What's up?

Kid: I forget to do it.

Parent: If you can't remember to feed the dog, then I can't remember to take you to gymnastics three times a week.

Parent: I've noticed that you haven't been too enthusiastic about riding the school bus lately. What's up?

Kid: The kids are being mean.

Parent: So stand up for yourself. The best defense is a good offense.

Possibility #2: He says nothing or "I don't know."

This is another possible way in which your kid might respond to your initial introduction to an unsolved problem. There are lots of reasons a kid might say nothing or "I don't know."

- *Your wording is off.* If you don't word unsolved problems according to the guidelines in chapter 4, you'll increase the likelihood of silence or "I don't know," often because your child doesn't completely understand what you're inquiring about or believes that he's in trouble or that you're mad. Perhaps you've only been talking with him about problems when you *are* mad or he *is* in trouble, so you'll want to reassure him that you're actually just trying to understand his concerns and solve the problem together.

- *Your timing is off.* Remember, Emergency Plan B adds heat and time pressure to the mix. Doing Plan B proactively so your child isn't surprised by your desire to have a discussion—and giving him some advance notice of the topic—can reduce the likelihood of "I don't know" and silence as well.

- *He really doesn't know* what his concern is about the problem you're trying to discuss. Perhaps you've never inquired about his concerns before, at least not in this way. Perhaps he's never given the matter any thought. Perhaps he's become so accustomed to having his concerns dismissed that he hasn't given thought to his concerns for a very long time.

- *He's had a lot of Plan A in his life, and he's still betting on the Plan A horse.* You'll have to prove to him—by solving problems collaboratively rather than unilaterally—that you're not riding that horse anymore. By the way, mere reassurance about that may not get the job done—the proof's in the pudding.

- *He may be reluctant to say what's on his mind.* Perhaps history has taught him that if he says what he thinks, you'll simply disagree or take offense and it'll cause a fight. Your goal in the Empathy step is to suspend your emotional response to what your child is saying, knowing that if you react emotionally to what you're hearing, he'll clam up and you won't end up hearing anything. You badly want to know your child's concerns, even if his concerns involve you.

- *He's buying time.* Many kids say "I don't know" instead of "Umm," or "Give me a second," or "Let me think about that a minute." Since you're not in a rush, you'll be able to give him a second and let him think about it a minute. Many kids say nothing because they're collecting their thoughts or because they're having difficulty putting their thoughts into words. Unfortunately, adults often respond to silence by filling the void with their own concerns, theories, or solutions. In such instances, you've strayed quite a bit from the main goals of the Empathy step (information gathering and understanding) and made it even more difficult for your kid to think. You may need to grow more comfortable with the silence that can occur as a kid is giving thought to his concerns.

If you've given your kid the chance to think and it's clear he really has no idea what his concerns are or is simply unable to put his thoughts into words, your best option is to do some educated guessing or hypothesis testing. Here, finally, your theories may actually come in handy. Suggest a few possibilities, based on experience, and see if any ring true:

Parent: I've noticed that you haven't been too enthusiastic about going to hockey lately. What's up?

Kid: I don't know.

Parent: Well, let's think about it. There's no rush.

Kid (after ten seconds): I really don't know.

Parent: Take your time.

Kid (after another five seconds): I really don't know.

Parent: Hmm. Well, I know some things you've told me before when you didn't want to go to hockey. Do you remember what those things were?

Kid: No.

Parent: Well, sometimes you're worried about making a mistake in front of the other kids. Is that it?

Kid: Kind of.

Parent: And you're worried that if you make a mistake, the other kids will get mad at you. Is that it too?

Kid: Yeah.

Parent: And you don't like it when Coach Dan yells at you. Is that happening?

Kid: Not so much.

Parent: So it's mainly that you're worried about being embarrassed and the kids getting mad at you if you make a mistake?

Kid: Uh-huh.

Parent: Anything else that we're not thinking of?

Kid: I don't think so.

Though that was a brief example, the kid's concern is now on the table. As you're in the midst of hypothesizing, bear in mind that you're proposing *possibilities* rather than divining the kid's concern. Here's what divining sounds like (this is an example of what *not* to do):

Parent: I've noticed that you haven't been too enthusiastic about going to hockey lately. What's up?

Kid: I don't know.

Parent: I think it's because you're worried about getting yelled at by Coach Dan.

Possibility #3:
He says, "I don't have a problem with that."

Many adults think that if their child says, "I don't have a problem with that," the game is over. After all, how can they talk with their child about a problem if their child says he doesn't have a problem with the problem? But this response isn't a dead end at all; indeed, it's usually the jumping-off point for learning more about his concern, perspective, or point of view. While it's entirely possible that he isn't as concerned about the problem as you are, that doesn't mean you can't proceed with Plan B. The first drilling strategy (reflective listening) should serve you well as an initial response.

Parent: I've noticed that you've been having difficulty getting along with your sister during dinner lately. What's up?

Kid: I don't have a problem with that.

Parent: Ah, you don't have a problem with that. I'm sorry—I'm not sure I understand what you mean.

Kid: I mean I don't really care if I get along with my sister.

Parent: Ah, you don't really care if you get along with your sister. Can you say more about that?

Kid: It doesn't really matter.

Parent: What do you mean?

Kid: She's just a little kid, and she's loud and annoying, and we're never going to get along.

Parent: She's just a little kid, she's loud and annoying, and you don't think you'll ever get along with her.

Kid: She's not going to stop being loud and annoying, I'm not going to stop thinking she's loud and annoying, so nothing's gonna change. It's hopeless. Plus, she knows she's your favorite. She can always complain to you and get me in trouble.

Sounds like he actually *does* have a problem with that (his sister is loud and annoying and gets him into trouble by complaining to Mom). By the way, even if a kid really isn't as concerned about the problem as you are, he's probably concerned about the *conflict* being caused by the problem. So there's still a problem to be solved.

Possibility #4:
He says, "I don't want to talk about it right now."

Fortunately, he doesn't have to talk about it right now, and it's a good idea to let him know that. Many kids start talking the instant they're given permission *not* to talk. If he truly doesn't want to talk about it right now, it's likely he has a good reason; maybe he'll talk about that. A lot of kids *will* talk about why they don't want to talk about something, which is very informative in its own right. Then, after they're through talking about that, they're comfortable enough to start talking about what they didn't want to talk about in the first place. Regrettably, many adults respond to a kid's reluctance to talk by *insisting harder* that the kid talk. But you don't want to try so hard to get your kid to talk today that you lose your credibility for tomorrow. There's always tomorrow. Many kids aren't going to talk until they're ready and able. I know quite a few adults who are the same way.

Possibility #5: He becomes defensive and says something like, "I don't have to talk to you" (or worse).

Let's think about why a kid would become defensive in response to adult requests for information on a particular unsolved problem. We've actually covered some of them already. Maybe he's accustomed to problems being solved unilaterally (Plan A). Maybe he thinks that if a problem is being raised, he must be in trouble, so he's anticipating excoriation and punishment. Maybe he doesn't really see the point in contemplating or voicing his concerns because he's become accustomed to having them swept off the table.

Fortunately, we're trying to break the patterns of communication and adult responses that would cause a kid to feel that talking is not his best option. Your best approach to defensive statements is not reciprocal defensiveness or threats of adult-imposed consequences but rather *honesty*. A good response to "I don't have to talk to you" would be "You don't have to talk to me." A good response to "You're not my boss" would be "I'm not trying to boss you." And a good response to "You can't make me talk" would be "I can't make you talk." Some reassurance that you're not using Plan A might be helpful, too, as in "I'm not telling you what to do" (you're not), "You're not in trouble" (he's not), "I'm not mad at you" (you're not), and "I'm just trying to understand" (you are). Statements like "I just want what's best for you" and "I'm doing this (imposing a solution) because I love you" would not be ideal.

You're ready to move on to the Define-Adult-Concerns step when you have a clear understanding of your kid's concern or perspective on a given unsolved problem. How do you know when you've reached that point? Keep summarizing and asking for more information (drilling strategy #8) until your child has no additional concerns.

THE DEFINE-ADULT-CONCERNS STEP:
REAL INFLUENCE
· · · · ·

Your child is not the only one with concerns. Based on your experience, wisdom, and values, you have valid, important concerns as well, and you want those concerns to be heard and taken into account. You want influence. Your time has come.

This step is made difficult primarily by the fact that adults often don't give much thought to their *concerns* about specific problems. Indeed, they often rush past their concerns and start proposing (and often imposing) their *solutions*. But solutions that are proposed before identifying the concerns of both parties won't work, since they can't possibly address those concerns. Power struggles—which you read about in chapter 3—result when you and your child are proposing *competing solutions* (solutions that do not address the concerns of both parties). There's no such thing as *competing concerns*, by the way— only different concerns that need to be addressed. The concerns of one party don't trump the concerns of the other, and the goal isn't to establish who's right and who's wrong. The concerns of both parties are of exactly equal legitimacy.

Are you saying my kid is my equal?

No, but if you want to solve problems collaboratively with your child, then his concerns are no less valid and meaningful than yours.

You'll need to give some careful thought to your concerns, and you can do that ahead of time if you're finding it hard to think about it in the moment. Simply restating the expectation your child is having difficulty meeting—"I'm concerned that you're not doing very well in math"—would *not* be an expression of your concerns. Rather, your concerns will almost always fall into one or both of two categories: (1) how the unsolved problem is affecting your child and/or (2) how the unsolved problem is affecting others.

Adult concerns usually begin with the words "The thing is . . ." or "My concern is . . ." but most definitely not "That is all well and good but . . ." Let's see what some typical adult concerns might be on some of the problems we've been discussing. At the end of each example you'll see a number designating the category (described in the previous paragraph) that the concerns fall into.

> Difficulty waking up in the morning: *My concern is that when you have difficulty waking up in the morning, you end up being late for school, and you're falling behind in your first two classes because you're frequently not there in time to attend them.* (1)
>
> Difficulty eating breakfast before school: *My concern is that*

you need energy to get your day off to a good start and I'm worried that when you don't eat breakfast, it makes it harder for you to focus on what's going on in your classes. (1)

Difficulty feeding the dog in the morning: *My concern is that if you forget to feed the dog, he will be hungry all day. (2)*

Difficulty riding the school bus: *The thing is, if you don't go to school on the school bus, then I have to take you to school and that makes me late for work, and my boss isn't too happy about that. (2)*

Difficulty answering cell phone: *The thing is, I worry about whether you're safe if I don't know where you are. (2)*

Difficulty understanding assignments in math: *My concern is that you're getting very discouraged about how you're doing in math and it's making it difficult for you to keep trying . . . and this year's math is the stepping stone to next year's math, so I'm concerned that next year is going to be even harder. (1)*

Let's now continue the example of Proactive Plan B we began previously. I'm including the entire dialogue because it may be useful to read the process sequentially:

The Empathy Step

Parent: I've noticed that you're having difficulty sticking with our thirty-minute time limit on electronics lately. What's up?

Max: It's not fair.

Parent: It's not fair. What's not fair?

Max: Thirty minutes isn't enough time.

Parent: Thirty minutes isn't enough time. How so?

Max: 'Cuz you think everything counts as electronics.

Parent: I think everything counts as electronics.

Max: You think Minecraft counts as electronics. And I agree with that. And you think playing Clash of Clans on my iPhone counts. And I agree with that too. But you also think texting counts. And you think Instagram counts. And you think Snapchat counts. If all that stuff is going to count, then thirty minutes isn't enough. So it's not fair.

Parent: So you feel that it's not fair for me to count all of those things as electronics.

Max: Yeah! I mean, I'm not even doing that much gaming! The thirty-minute time limit was supposed to be just for gaming. But now you're counting everything with a screen as part of the thirty minutes!

Parent: And you feel that things that aren't gaming shouldn't count.

Max: No! I mean, those other things are how kids communicate these days. That's how I communicate with my friends. So if those things count as electronics time, then I wouldn't have any time left for gaming.

Parent: I get it. So when I'm telling you to get off your cell phone or the computer, what are you thinking?

Max: I'm thinking you're the only parent I know who thinks that other stuff counts as screen time. And I'm thinking it's not fair. And I'm thinking I wish you knew more about how kids communicate these days.

Parent: So you feel that it's not fair that there's a thirty-minute limit on electronics; and you feel that the stuff you're doing on a screen besides gaming shouldn't count as part of the thirty minutes;

and you feel that most other parents don't think that stuff should count as screen time. Is there anything else I should know about what's getting in the way of you sticking with the thirty-minute limit on screen time?

Max: Well, you kind of freak out when you see my phone next to me when I'm doing my homework. I can text my friends while I'm doing my homework and still get my homework done. Sometimes I'm texting them about the homework.

Parent: OK. Although you have told me that the texting sometimes distracts you when you're doing your homework.

Max: Yeah, sometimes, but not most of the time. Plus, if it's distracting me, I just don't pay attention to it until my homework's done.

The Define-Adult-Concerns Step

Parent: My concern is that I don't always know what you're doing on your phone or on your computer, so I don't know how much time you're really spending on gaming. And I think all that electronic stuff is keeping you awake later at night and keeping you from hanging out with me and Dad and Molly.

Both sets of concerns are now on the table. No turning back now.

THE INVITATION STEP:
COLLABORATING ON SOLUTIONS
· · · · ·

This final step involves considering potential solutions that will address the concerns of both parties, concerns that have been identified and clarified in the first two steps. It's called the Invitation step because you're actually inviting your child to collaborate on solutions together. The Invitation lets your child know that solving the problem is something you're doing *with* him (collaboratively) rather than *to* him (unilaterally).

To start this step, you could simply say something like, "Let's think about how we can solve this problem," or "Let's think about how we can work that out." But to facilitate the consideration of solutions that will address the concerns of both parties, it's usually better to recap the concerns that were identified in the first two steps, usually starting with the words "I wonder if there's a way . . ." So, for the aforementioned example, that would sound something like this: "I wonder if there's a way for you to use your phone and computer to communicate with your friends without it counting as screen time"—that was the kid's concern—"but for me to make sure that you're sticking with the thirty-minute limit on gaming, that you're getting to bed on time, and that you're still hanging out with us sometimes" (those were the adult's concerns).

Then you give your child the first opportunity to propose a solution: "Do you have any ideas?" This is not an indication that the burden for solving the problem is placed solely on your child. The burden for solving the problem is placed on the problem-solving team (you and your child). But giving your kid the first crack at thinking of a solution is a good strategy for letting him know you're actually interested in his ideas. It also gives him practice at thinking of solutions. Too often we assume that the only person capable of coming up with a good solution to a problem is the adult. While there is a chance that your kid won't be able to think of any solutions, it's actually quite likely that he *can* think of solutions, and even ones that will take your combined concerns into account.

There's also a good chance he has been waiting, perhaps not so patiently, for you to give him the chance.

Many parents enter Plan B with a preordained solution. In other words, they already know where the Plan B plane is landing before it takes off. If you already know where the plane is landing before it takes off, then you're not using Plan B—you're using a "clever" form of Plan A. Plan B is not just a "clever" form of Plan A. Plan B is collaborative. Plan A is unilateral.

The reality is that there is no flight plan. The Plan B plane will head wherever the crosswinds of your combined concerns take you. But you do have some gauges in the cockpit to help you and your collaborative partner know where to land the plane: the solution must be *realistic* (meaning both parties can actually do what they're agreeing to do) and *mutually satisfactory* (meaning the solution truly and logically addresses the concerns of both parties). If a solution isn't realistic and mutually satisfactory, alternative solutions should be generated and considered. By the way, "trying harder" is never a viable solution.

The realistic part is important because Plan B isn't an exercise in wishful thinking. If you can't execute your part of the solution that's under consideration, don't agree to it just to end the conversation. Likewise, if you don't think your kid can execute his part of the solution that's under consideration, then try to get him to take a moment to think about whether he can actually do what he's agreeing to do ("You sure you can do that? Let's make sure we come up with a solution we can both do").

The mutually satisfactory part is important, too, and requires that you and your child give conscious, deliberate thought to the concerns the solution is intended to address. In other words, all proposed solutions are evaluated on the basis of whether they address the concerns identified in the first two steps of Plan B. The mutually satisfactory aspect is a great comfort to adults who fear that in using Plan B their concerns will go unaddressed and no limits will be set. *You're "setting limits" if your concerns are being addressed. If a solution is mutually satisfactory, then by definition your concerns have been addressed.* If you thought that Plan A is the only mechanism by which adults can set limits, you were mistaken.

The mutually satisfactory part also helps the kid know that *you're as invested in ensuring that his concerns are addressed as you are in making sure that yours are addressed.* That's how you lose an enemy and gain a problem-solving partner. That's how you move from adversary to teammate.

Early on, your child may come up with solutions that address *his* concerns but not *yours.* You may have the same tendency. That doesn't mean he's come up with a bad idea—or that he doesn't care about your concerns or is unable to take them into account—only that he's not yet highly skilled at coming up with solutions that are mutually satisfactory. Simply remind him that the goal is to come up with a solution that works for both of you, perhaps by saying, "Well, that's an idea, and I know that idea would address your concern, but I don't think it would address my concern. Let's see if we can come up with an idea that will work for both of us."

Many parents, in their eagerness to solve the problem, forget the Invitation step. This means that just as they are at the precipice of actually collaborating on a solution, they impose a solution. Not good. Your kid thought you were partnering with him in solving a problem and then you went back to being unilateral and pulled the collaborative rug out from under him. He's likely to have major reservations about participating in the process again the next time.

Let's see how the three ingredients would go together, assuming that things are going smoothly. Again, forgive the redundancy, but it's helpful to see the process unfold from start to finish.

The Empathy Step

Parent: I've noticed that you're having difficulty sticking with our thirty-minute time limit on electronics lately. What's up?

Max: It's not fair.

Parent: It's not fair. What's not fair?

Max: Thirty minutes isn't enough time.

Parent: Thirty minutes isn't enough time. How so?

Max: 'Cuz you think everything counts as electronics.

Parent: I think everything counts as electronics.

Max: You think Minecraft counts as electronics. And I agree with that. And you think playing Clash of Clans on my iPhone counts. And I agree with that too. But you also think texting counts. And you think Instagram counts. And you think Snapchat counts. If all that stuff is going to count, then thirty minutes isn't enough. So it's not fair.

Parent: So you feel that it's not fair for me to count all of those things as electronics.

Max: Yeah! I mean, I'm not even doing that much gaming! The thirty-minute time limit was supposed to be just for gaming. But now you're counting everything with a screen as part of the thirty minutes!

Parent: And you feel that things that aren't gaming shouldn't count.

Max: No! I mean, those other things are how kids communicate these days. That's how I communicate with my friends. So if those things count as electronics time, then I wouldn't have any time left for gaming.

Parent: I get it. So when I'm telling you to get off your cell phone or the computer, what are you thinking?

Max: I'm thinking you're the only parent I know who thinks that other stuff counts as screen time. And I'm thinking it's not fair. And I'm thinking I wish you knew more about how kids communicate these days.

Parent: So you feel that it's not fair that there's a thirty-minute limit on electronics; and you feel that the stuff you're doing on a screen besides gaming shouldn't count as part of the thirty minutes; and you feel that most other parents don't think that stuff should count as screen time. Is there anything else I should know about what's getting in the way of you sticking with the thirty-minute limit on screen time?

Max: Well, you kind of freak out when you see my phone next to me when I'm doing my homework. I can text my friends while I'm doing my homework and still get my homework done. Sometimes I'm texting them about the homework.

Parent: OK. Although you have told me that the texting sometimes distracts you when you're doing your homework.

Max: Yeah, sometimes, but not most of the time. Plus, if it's distracting me, I just don't pay attention to it until my homework's done.

The Define-Adult-Concerns Step

Parent: My concern is that I don't always know what you're doing on your phone or on your computer, so I don't know how much time you're really spending on gaming. And I think all that electronic stuff is keeping you awake later at night and keeping you from hanging out with me and Dad and Molly.

The Invitation Step

Parent: I wonder if there's a way for us to make sure you get your thirty minutes of game time every day . . . and still connect with your friends through Snapchat and Instagram and texting . . . but in a way that let's me know you're only gaming for the thirty minutes . . . and doesn't keep you awake at night . . . and doesn't keep you from hanging out with me and Dad and Molly. Do you have any ideas?

Max: No.

Parent: Well, let's think about it. I bet we can solve this problem.

Max: Well, I usually do gaming right after I get home from school or from football practice because I need some downtime. So, like, we could have a set time for gaming so you'll know that's what I'm doing.

Parent: That's an interesting idea. I didn't know that's when you mostly do your games.

Max: Well, sometimes I do it after I'm done with my homework if I haven't had a chance to do any gaming before that. And weekends are different. I do gaming when I wake up in the morning on weekends.

Parent: And do you think you stick to the thirty-minute limit on gaming on weekend mornings? It seems like you're gaming way more than that.

Max: Um . . . you're probably right. But I think I should have a little more time to do gaming on weekends, since I have more free time.

Parent: Thanks for your honesty. I can think about the extra time for gaming on weekends. But let's get back to weekdays. How will I know when you're gaming?

Max: I really only do it after school or after homework. And it's not

111

usually after homework, because I usually finish my homework so late that I go right to bed when I'm done.

Parent: To tell you the truth, I've never been a big fan of gaming right before bed. I think it makes it hard for you to fall asleep.

Max: Can I do texting and Instagram and Snapchat before I go to bed . . . you know, so I can, like, connect with my friends one last time?

Parent: I don't have a problem with that, so long as it doesn't keep you from going to sleep. So how do we keep track of how much time you're connecting with your friends?

Max: Um . . . I don't know how we'd keep track of that. I only do it for, like, a minute or two at a time, but I do it a lot of times every day.

Parent: But don't you have games on your iPhone? How will I know you're only connecting with your friends when you're on your iPhone?

Max: I don't mind taking the games off my iPhone. All I have on there is a flight simulator and Clash of Clans, and I'm kind of getting sick of those.

Parent: That would be good. And can we have a time that the iPhone gets put away at night?

Max: How about fifteen minutes after I finish my homework I turn off my iPhone?

Parent: I can deal with that. And no games on your iPhone. And gaming only right after you get home from school or from football practice. And I won't bug you about how much you're on your iPhone. Wow, we're doing pretty well here. Thanks for talking with me about this.

Max: We just have two more things to solve.

Parent: We do?

Max: Yeah. Weekend gaming . . . and the part about my electronics keeping me from being with you and Dad and Molly.

Parent: Yes, I forgot about that part. Thanks, Max.

Max: Can we talk about those tomorrow? I think I'm kinda worn out.

Parent: Yes, we can talk about those tomorrow. I might be kinda worn out myself.

Max: But I don't think it's going to be hard to solve the spending-time one, because if I'm gaming right after school or football practice, that's not a time when you and Dad and Molly are even doing stuff that you want me to be a part of.

Parent: I think that's true. I guess I'm just thinking about all the times we're together—especially on the weekends—and you have your face in your iPhone. But let's save that one for tomorrow. And let's see how our solutions work for our other problems. If they don't work, we'll talk about them some more.

That last line was important, as it underscores a very important point: it's good for you and your child to acknowledge that the problem may require additional discussion, because there's actually a decent chance that *the first solution won't solve the problem durably*. Why wouldn't the first solution solve the problem durably? Often because it wasn't as realistic or mutually satisfactory as it first seemed. Or because the first attempt at clarifying concerns yielded useful but incomplete information. By definition, the solution will only address the concerns you know about, but it can't possibly address the ones you haven't heard about yet. And because solving a problem in real life isn't usually a one-and-done affair. Good solutions—durable ones—are usually refined versions of the solutions that came before them.

Are you thinking that our first example of all three steps of Plan B went rather seamlessly? You're right—it was pretty smooth sailing. It's good to see an initial example of all three steps without major glitches. We'll be getting around to glitches in the next chapter.

Q & A

Question: I'm still a little confused about Plan A. It seems like I'm not supposed to tell my child what to do anymore.

Answer: That's a common point of confusion. Remember, Plan A is when you're *imposing a solution to an unsolved problem*. But, as you've read, that's not the same thing as voicing your expectations. So, "I'd like you to set the dinner table," is not Plan A. Nor is "Please stop teasing your sister," or "I think you need to be a little more aggressive going after the puck in hockey." You're still very much in the business of making your expectations known. But if you find that you're telling your kid to do the same things over and over, you might want to consider whether repeated telling is really your most effective strategy.

Question: So is everything a negotiation?

Answer: Plan B isn't best thought of as negotiating or even compromising. Plan B is solving problems collaboratively. Remember, your child is already meeting many of your expectations. Plan B is for the expectations he's having difficulty meeting.

Question: I've been using a lot of Plan A, and now I understand why that's not ideal. But Plan B is going to be quite a change for me. Thoughts?

Answer: It may take a while for you to get comfortable with and proficient at solving problems collaboratively and proactively. Early on, it may feel like you're giving up some control of your child. Of course, you probably didn't have as much control as you thought anyway, and hopefully you're not viewing control in such a positive light anymore. But solving problems collaboratively can also be a great relief. You're off the hook for coming up with instantaneous, ingenious solutions to the problems your child encounters. In addition, the problems affecting your child's life are no longer a source of conflict between you and him. Making the shift is a lot easier if you're being *proactive* rather than *reactive*; again, it's harder to stay away from Plan A in the heat of the moment.

Question: Doesn't Plan B take a lot more time than Plan A?
Answer: That's a pretty common initial reaction to Plan B. Though it may have felt like coming up with a quick, unilateral solution to a problem was a time-saver, unilateral solutions usually don't work and therefore take an enormous amount of time.

Question: There's a lot going on in Plan B besides solving problems, yes?
Answer: Yes, indeed. As you've read, Plan B is how relationships are built (or rebuilt) and communication enhanced (or restored). It's how you and your child learn about his skills, beliefs, values, preferences, personality traits, goals, and direction, along with your values, wisdom, and experience. It's how you have influence without the use of power. It's how—and

we haven't really talked much about this yet, and won't until chapter 9—you bring out the best in you and your child and foster the qualities on the more positive side of human nature.

Question: The Empathy step reminds me a little of something I read in Stephen Covey's 7 *Habits of Highly Effective People* . . . am I on to something?

Answer: You are. In that book, Mr. Covey points out that we spend years learning how to read and write and speak but have probably had very little training in listening:

If you're like most people, you probably seek first to be understood; you want to get your point across. And in doing so, you may ignore the other person completely, pretend that you're listening, selectively hear only certain parts of the conversation or attentively focus on only the words being said, but miss the meaning entirely. So why does this happen? Because most people listen with the intent to reply, not to understand. You listen to yourself as you prepare in your mind what you are going to say, the questions you are going to ask, etc. You filter everything you hear through your life experiences, your frame of reference. You check what you hear against your autobiography and see how it measures up. And consequently, you decide prematurely what the other person means before he/she finishes communicating.

Question: Will my kid start talking to me again if I approach problems with Plan B? I miss him.

Answer: If he comes to recognize that you're going to listen to, clarify, and validate his concerns, and that those concerns will be addressed, you've certainly laid the foundation for him to start talking to you again. Perhaps he misses you too.

Question: Will he start listening to my concerns too?
Answer: Kids whose concerns are heard and addressed—rather than dismissed or ignored—are far more interested in hearing your concerns and in making sure that they are addressed too.

Question: So if I notice that my child is having difficulty meeting a particular expectation, when should I try to solve the problem? Immediately?
Answer: It probably depends on the unsolved problem. If he just brought home his first bad grade on a spelling test, you don't necessarily need to intervene immediately. One option is to watch closely to see if your kid is making independent progress toward improving the spelling grade (Plan C). You want to promote independence at virtually every step along the way. But if he's not making independent progress, you also don't want him to struggle for too long. If you don't intervene when it's become clear he's unable to overcome incompatibility on his own, he'll lose faith in his ability to surmount hurdles. Letting kids drown isn't the ideal way for them to learn to swim.

Question: Can you say more about Plan C? Somehow setting aside an unsolved problem makes me feel like I'm dropping all of my expectations.

Answer: Remember, there are different reasons for using Plan C: (1) you've concluded you don't really care that much about a given expectation; (2) you've decided to defer to your child's skills, beliefs, values, preferences, personality traits, and goals; (3) you've decided to let your child try to solve the problem independently, at least for now; (4) you've concluded that the expectation is unrealistic for your child at this point in his development; or (5) you have other higher-priority expectations to pursue. But you're definitely not dropping all of your expectations. You're still working on some unsolved problems with Plan B. Don't forget, there are many expectations your child is already meeting.

Question: I've always believed that most people—kids included—are inherently selfish. Aren't we all primarily interested in making sure that our own concerns are addressed?

Answer: There's no question, we all (kids included) want to make sure our concerns are heard and addressed. And yes, we tend to be more passionate about and devoted to our own concerns than we are to the concerns of others. But that doesn't mean we're devoted to ensuring that our concerns are addressed *to the exclusion of the concerns of others*. I'm always amazed—and I get daily reminders of this—at how willing kids are to take the concerns of others into account in formulating solutions. They just need practice at it. If imposition of adult will is the primary way in which adults exert their influence, neither the kids nor the adults get that practice, and the kids just perpetuate the cycle.

The problems we humans grapple with—and not just

those between adults and kids—demand that we hear each other's concerns and work together toward durable, mutually satisfactory solutions. We need each other. We need to do it together.

. . . . .

Let's see what Plan B looks like in one of the families we've been following.

Denise decided to give Plan B a try when she was putting Charlotte to bed one night. This was their "mushy time," and the boys, who were downstairs watching a TV show, were unlikely to interrupt.

Denise sat down next to Charlotte on her bed. "Charlotte, can I talk with you about something?"

"Yes, Mommy. Is something wrong?"

My sensitive one, thought Denise. "No, nothing's wrong. I just thought you and I could solve a problem together. Wanna try?"

"What kind of problem?"

"Well, I meant to tell you earlier that I wanted to talk to you about it. It's about getting out of the house on time for school. Can we talk about that?"

"OK. Are you mad?"

"No, I'm not mad at all. But I've noticed that it's hard for you to get ready for school in the morning on time to catch the school bus. What's up?"

"I don't like rushing in the morning," Charlotte replied.

Denise didn't quite understand this response. But safe in the knowledge that mind reading is not a prerequisite for solving problems collaboratively, she did some reflective listening. "You don't like rushing in the morning. I don't understand what you mean."

"I don't like having to pick out my clothes and take a shower and eat breakfast and feed the dog all in a rush. It's too much for me to do. There's not enough time."

Denise felt like telling Charlotte that there would be plenty of time if she didn't get distracted by the TV, but resisted the temptation. She did some more reflective listening instead. "So there's not enough time."

"No, and that's why I sometimes forget to feed the dog."

"Because you're in such a rush and there's too many things for you to do."

"Yes."

"Is there anything else making it hard for you to get ready for school in the morning in time to catch the school bus?"

"I also like when you drive me to school. So we can have time together."

This one Denise had heard before. "Yes, I know you like spending time with me when I drive you to school in the morning."

"'Cuz the boys aren't with us."

"Ah, because the boys aren't with us. So that makes it especially nice."

"Yes."

Denise noticed that the tenderness she was feeling for her daughter at this moment was in sharp contrast with how she felt most weekday mornings when Charlotte was running late. She decided to summarize the territory they'd already covered. "So, one of the reasons that you have trouble getting ready for school in the morning is because you feel you don't have enough time to do everything. And another reason is that you like when I drive you to school because the boys aren't with us and it's nice for us to spend some time together without them."

Charlotte nodded.

"Are there any other reasons you have trouble getting ready for school in the morning in time to catch the school bus?"

Charlotte shook her head. "Are we done talking now?"

"Why? Do you want to be done talking now?"

"No. I like talking to you, Mommy."

"Oh good; well, we're not quite done talking yet. We still need to solve the problem. See, my concern is that I'm very busy in the morning—you know, getting everybody's breakfast ready and getting myself ready for work too. So it makes it a little hard for me when I have to keep track of everything you're supposed to be doing, because I have so much to do in the morning myself. Do you understand what I mean?"

Charlotte clutched her rag doll. "I'm sorry, Mommy."

"Oh, no need to be sorry, honey. I just thought maybe we could think about how to solve the problem."

"What problem?"

"You know, you having a lot to do in the morning . . . and wanting to spend time together without the boys . . . and me having so much to keep track of in the morning that it's hard for me to keep track of you. Do you have any ideas?"

Charlotte pondered the question. "Could you feed Skipper in the morning? And I could feed Skipper at night?"

Denise considered this proposal. "That would help you have less to do in the morning?"

"Yes. But I could feed him at night when you usually feed him. Because I don't have any chores at night."

"That's an interesting idea, Charlotte. I think I like it. So we'd just swap what time we're both going to feed him. You'd remember to feed Skipper at night?"

"I could feed him right when I get home from day care. He's always hungry then."

"We could try that. Any other ideas?"

"I could get up fifteen minutes early," Charlotte proposed. "Like when you get up." Charlotte often ended up in Denise's bed in the middle of the night, so she was well aware of Denise's movements in the morning. "Then I'd have more time. I'm awake anyways."

"So you'd get up when I get up?"

"Uh-huh. And maybe I could take my shower at night so I wouldn't have to do it in the morning. That would save time too. And maybe I could pick out my clothes the night before too so I wouldn't have to do that in the morning either."

Denise looked at Charlotte with some amazement. It often occurred to her that her daughter was wise well beyond her years. "These are really good ideas, Charlotte. So let's think: you'd pick out your clothes the night before, and you'd take a shower the night before too. And you'd get out of bed fifteen minutes earlier when I do." Denise reflected on whether all of this was realistic. "I think that might work very well."

"And maybe I could eat my breakfast in front of the TV when I'm all ready for school."

Ah, the dreaded TV, thought Denise. *But if Charlotte could get everything done, I don't mind her eating breakfast in front of the TV.* "So, let's think about how that would work. You'd come downstairs and I'd have your breakfast ready, and if you were all ready for school, you'd get to eat breakfast in front of the TV?"

Charlotte nodded.

"Should we start this plan tomorrow?" Denise asked.

"OK."

"Now, there's one more part of what we talked about that we haven't really done anything about yet."

Charlotte looked puzzled.

"The part about you wanting to spend time with me by yourself," Denise reminded.

"Oh, yeah."

"How could we solve that problem?"

"I don't know," said Charlotte.

"Because it's kind of tough for me to take you to school in the car in the morning," said Denise. "It's hard for me to get to work on time if I take you to school."

"Could we find another time that's just you and me?" volunteered Charlotte.

Denise quickly reflected on how she was stretched for time already. But this little kid of hers wanted to spend more time with her, and she was determined to find a way. "Well, we spend time together when I take you to Daddy's apartment," said Denise. "And you go food shopping with me a lot. And I put you to bed every night just you and me."

Charlotte nodded. "But I love my mommy."

"So should we figure out another time that we could spend time together, just you and me?"

"On your weekends could we play with my dolls together? Daddy doesn't play with dolls."

"You mean on the weekends when you're not at Daddy's? We'd find a time to play dolls together?"

"Uh-huh."

"That's something you'd like me to do with you?"

"Yes. It's more fun than playing with them alone."

"I think that would be a very good thing for us to do together. Shall we try to find time to do that this weekend?"

Charlotte nodded. "Are we done talking now, Mommy?"

"I think we are."

Denise and Charlotte read a book together. Then Denise kissed Charlotte good night, turned off the light, and went into the living room to get bedtime rolling with Nick. (Hank had decided years ago that he was too old for his mother to put him to bed at night, so he usually went to bed on his own at 9:30 p.m.) But buoyed by the success of her first Plan B with Charlotte, she decided to give it a try with Hank as well.

"Hank, can I talk with you about something before you go to sleep tonight?" Denise asked, interrupting Hank's double-screening (using Instagram on his smartphone and watching *Shark Tank* on TV).

"About what?" Hank grunted, not looking away from either screen.

Ah, my surly one, thought Denise. "About how you get along with your brother and sister."

"I don't care about how I get along with my brother and sister. They're annoying."

Well, this is a horse of a different color, Denise thought, though she wasn't surprised. "Hank, you're not in trouble. I just want to get your take on things."

"My take on things is that they're annoying and you're making it hard for me to watch *Shark Tank*."

Denise decided that this was a losing proposition for now. "Well, it is something I want to talk with you about at some point. So I'll talk with you later about a good time to do that."

"Never would be a good time to do that," said Hank, as he turned the volume up on the TV.

There are a few takeaways from this story. First, there's a good chance that the same solution won't address all of the concerns you hear about in the Empathy step. For example, in the case of Denise and Charlotte, the same solution wouldn't address Charlotte's two primary concerns (having a lot to do in the morning and wanting to spend time together without the boys). So you'll want to come up with separate solutions to both concerns, possibly in separate Plan B discussions.

Second, if you were a bit taken aback by Hank's initial response to Denise's efforts to talk with him and felt that he needed a quick lesson on respecting one's elders, you may want to hold off on that. Hank's response may simply have been borne of his having been interrupted, but it may also reflect a pattern of interactions that have evolved over several years. A quick lesson on respect won't fix that; continued use of Plan B is a better bet.

- Chapter 6 -

TECHNICAL SUPPORT

Now that you have a general sense of what's involved in solving problems collaboratively, it would probably be good for you to be aware of some of the ways in which Plan B can go off the rails. That'll help you keep things on track. So this chapter is mostly about what *not* to do. By the way, these pitfalls will make the most sense once you've actually tried to do Plan B with your child.

Old Instincts: When the Going Gets Rough, You Still Head for Plan A
· · · · ·

Many adults automatically start thinking of the solutions and consequences they can impose when their child isn't meeting a particular expectation. Of course, there's nothing that says you have to follow your first instinct. It may be helpful to think things through a little so as to consider whether Plan A is really your best option. Here's what that might sound like in your head:

Maya has fallen behind in her classes again. I need to ground her so she can get her work done. I mean, why the heck is she going to yoga at night if she's behind in her classes? I need to lay down the law. This is the semester colleges are going to be looking at the most! How can she not know that? On the other hand, she was out sick three days last week, and that's why she's behind. And she's always gotten caught up when she's fallen behind before. So maybe I don't need to ground her. But, really, yoga? Well, maybe it's not so terrible that she needs a break from all that schoolwork. But how am I going to make sure she's getting caught up? I guess I could talk to her about it . . .

When You Assume: Entering the Empathy Step
Thinking You Already Know Your Child's
Concern or Perspective

· · · · ·

As you've read, parents are often quite certain they already know what their children's concerns are. Then they impose solutions based on those assumptions. Because those assumptions are often incorrect, those solutions are doomed. So you may want to strive for something we'll call Assumption-Free Living. Assumption-Free Living is liberating. It releases you from the distraction and false certainty of your assumptions and frees you to actually *find out* what's going on with your kid. By asking her. For many parents, a common experience in the Empathy step is learning the truth of the famous maxim about *what happens when you assume*. It's not a catastrophe to have some hypotheses about your child's concerns on a particular unsolved problem, so long as you also bear in mind that those hypotheses may be incorrect and, at the very least, are awaiting confirmation. The trick is to keep your hypotheses on the back burner while you're drilling for information. Otherwise, you're at risk of perfunctory drilling and/or of steering the discussion toward a predetermined destination.

Too Much Ingenuity: Entering Plan B with a Preordained Solution

· · · · ·

There are many adults who think it's in the parental job description to be the one to come up with solutions to the problems that affect their child's life. After all, we know best. Except that we often don't know best, especially when we have insufficient information from our Problem-Solving Partner. Solutions that are viable and durable are those that address the concerns of both parties, and you can't address the concerns of both parties if you don't know what those concerns are. That's why the Empathy step and the Define-Adult-Concerns step come before the Invitation. It's fine to have some ideas for how a problem can be solved, but it's important to remember that the litmus test for all solutions is the degree to which they are realistic and address the concerns of both parties.

Bad Timing: Relying on Emergency Plan B Instead of Proactive Plan B

· · · · ·

Solving problems proactively can be a major challenge for busy parents. However, there's not much choice but to carve out the time. As you know, Emergency Plan B involves more heat and less ideal circumstances (e.g., you're driving the car, trying to leave the house, or in the middle of the grocery store and have other kids and people around). Plus, solutions arrived at through Emergency Plan B tend to be stopgap rather than durable. Remember, you're trying to come up with solutions that solve the problem durably, not solutions that simply get you over the hump for the day. That's why you want to identify unsolved problems and prioritize ahead of time.

As you also know, even when you're using Plan B proactively, you'd be well served to give your kid some advance notice of the problem you'd like to discuss. Otherwise, she may still respond like you've sprung the problem on her with no warning.

Act of Desperation:
Using Plan B as a Last Resort
· · · · ·

You want Plan B to become the *norm* for solving problems in your family, not the exception. Plan B isn't something you turn to only when exhorting and extorting has failed.

At a Loss for Words:
Drilling Can Be Hard
· · · · ·

It's not always easy to know what to say to keep your kid talking so you can get the information you're seeking. You'll want to rely on the drilling strategies you read about in chapter 5; they really do help. But there are also some things kids say in response to "What's up?" that can leave you at a loss. Some examples:

Parent: I've noticed you've been having difficulty getting your vocabulary words done lately. What's up?

Kid: It's boring.

Parent (trying to drill): What's boring about it?

Kid: It's just boring.

Parent: I've noticed you haven't been eating what I've been making for dinner lately. What's up?

Kid: I don't like it.

Parent (trying to drill): What don't you like about it?

Kid: It doesn't taste right.

Parent (still trying to drill): Well, can you tell me what doesn't taste right?

Kid: It just doesn't taste right.

Yes, there are kids who instantaneously begin expressing their concerns when you present them with an unsolved problem, but if your kid isn't one of them, stick with the drilling strategies. Remember, your default drilling option is reflective listening. Let's see what this drilling strategy (and others) might look like in situations in which the Empathy step gets off to a slow start. These dialogues don't take you all the way through Plan B; they just show you how drilling perseverance can get you some traction:

Parent: I've noticed you've been having difficulty getting your vocabulary words done lately. What's up?

Kid: It's boring.

Parent (trying to drill, using strategy #2): What's boring about it?

Kid: It's just boring.

Parent (perhaps looking at those drilling strategies in chapter 5 and deciding on strategy #4): Hmm. So when you're sitting there trying to do the vocabulary words, what are you thinking?

Kid: I'm thinking it's boring.

Parent (strategies #1 and #4): Ah, you're thinking it's boring. What else are you thinking?

Kid: I'm thinking I'm not going to remember the definitions for the quiz the next day.

Parent (strategy #1): Ah, you're thinking you're not going to be able to remember the definitions for the quiz the next day.

Kid: I never do. That's why my English grade isn't that good. I never get good grades on the vocab quizzes.

Parent: I didn't know that. I'd like to hear more about that . . .

Good, some traction. Naturally, the conversation would continue from there. Here's another:

Parent: I've noticed you haven't been eating what I've been making for dinner lately. What's up?

Kid: It doesn't taste right.

Parent (using strategy #2): What doesn't taste right?

Kid: It just doesn't taste right.

Parent (using strategy #3): You know, I noticed that some nights you eat what I make and some nights you don't. Are there some things I make that you like and some things I make that you don't?

Kid: I like chicken nuggets.

Parent: Yes, I've noticed that you do like chicken nuggets. But I think there are other things I make that you eat.

Kid: Like what?

Parent: Pasta.

Kid: Oh, yeah, pasta. But only with butter. Not with red sauce. And not with meat.

Parent: What don't you like about the red sauce and the meat?

Kid: The meat is disgusting. And the red sauce just doesn't taste right.

Parent: Anything else I make that you like?

Kid: No.

Parent: Sometimes you like oatmeal.

Kid: Not when you put raisins or nuts in it.

Parent: Anything I make that you especially don't like?

Kid: I don't like the vegetables . . . except mashed potatoes.

Parent: I'm glad we're figuring out what you like and don't like. That'll help us solve this problem.

Misplaced Skepticism: Your Kid Verbalizes Her Concern or Perspective in the Empathy Step, but You Don't Believe Her
• • • • •

While it's conceivable that your kid's first stab at identifying and articulating her concerns may not be spot-on—she may not have given her concerns much thought until you asked—many adults are quick to view a kid's concerns as wrong or untrue. Sometimes this is because her concerns don't coincide with your preconceived notions. But your kid's concerns *can't* be wrong or untrue, because there's no such thing as wrong or untrue concerns. Her point of view is as legitimate as yours, though it may need some clarifying. For example, some kids may feel embarrassed about their concern or perspective or may be worried about how you'll respond, but that's not lying. So the last thing you'd want to do is dismiss her concerns or, worse, tell her you think she's lying. Then she'll stop talking to you. When you're solving problems collaboratively, you don't really have to worry about lying, which is quite a shift from feeling like you need to be on constant guard against being played for a fool or having the wool pulled over your eyes. When kids recognize that they're not in trouble and that you're purely interested in understanding their concern, perspective, or point of view on a given unsolved problem, they don't have much incentive to fabricate. The tone you're setting in the Empathy step isn't accusatory, nor is it adversarial or confrontational. Your kid isn't in trouble. You're not mad. The tone is one of *curiosity*. You really want to understand.

When adults think a kid is lying in the Empathy step, it's often because the adult isn't inquiring about a specific unsolved problem but rather about a *behavior* someone saw the kid exhibit, usually setting the stage for an exercise in *grilling* rather than drilling. Here's what that sounds like (notice the adult isn't really doing the Empathy step):

Parent: I heard from your teacher, Ms. Fornier, that you kicked Victor on the playground.

Kid: I did not.

Parent: Now, why would Ms. Fornier make that up?

Kid: I don't know, but she is. I didn't kick him. He kicked me.

Parent: That's not what she said.

Kid: Well, she's wrong.

Parent: She said she saw it with her own eyes!

Kid: Then she's blind, 'cuz I didn't kick him. Why don't you believe me?

Whether the kid and Ms. Fornier are accurately recounting the episode is one issue. But trying to get to the bottom of a *specific episode* is beside the point anyway, because what happened in that episode isn't nearly as important as solving the *chronic problem* of the kid and Victor having difficulty getting along on the playground.

Who Cares? Your Child Says She Doesn't Care about Your Concern, so Your Enthusiasm for Plan B Dissipates Rapidly

· · · · ·

Don't be insulted that she doesn't care about your concern. Let's face it: you may not actually care that much about hers. The good news is that she doesn't really have to *care* about your concern; she just has to take it into *account* as you pursue a mutually satisfactory solution together. She'll start trying to address your concerns not too long after you start trying to address hers. Here's an example:

Parent: Jackson, I've noticed that it's been difficult for you to come to dinner when you're playing your video games. What's up?

Jackson: You always make me quit in the middle of a game.

Parent: I always make you quit in the middle of a game. Good to know. Tell me, what game are you usually in the middle of playing?

Jackson: Madden.

Parent: Ah, Madden. You play that a lot.

Jackson: I like Madden.

Parent: I know you do. So sometimes you're in the middle of a Madden game. Tell me, does the Madden game pause so you can come back to it later?

Jackson: Yeah.

Parent: What's hard about pausing the game so you can come back to it later?

Jackson: You don't let me go back to it later. You make me do homework right after dinner. So then I can't go back to finish the game.

Parent: Now I understand. Is there anything else that's hard about coming to dinner when you're playing Madden?

Jackson: No.

Parent: OK. Well, the thing is, it's really important to me that we eat dinner together as a family. Because that's really the only time during the day that we get to be together and talk to each other.

Jackson: I don't care if we eat dinner together as a family.

Parent: Um . . . OK. Well, I guess it's probably more important to me that we eat together than it is to you. But I'm thinking that if we could get the problem solved in a way that works for both of us, then we could get it solved once and for all and then we wouldn't keep fighting about it.

You're Asking Me? Your Kid Doesn't
Have Any Ideas for Solutions
· ʼ · · ·

Hopefully you have some ideas. Remember, it's not her job to solve the problem; it's the job of the Problem-Solving Partners: you and her. If your kid truly has no ideas, it's fine for you to offer some proposals, so long as you don't end up imposing a solution in the process. In other words, no matter who proposes the solution, it still needs to be realistic and mutually satisfactory.

Premature Consummation: Rolling With Solutions
that Aren't Realistic and Mutually Satisfactory
· · · · ·

Once a solution is proposed, you and your child should give deliberate thought to whether the solution under consideration is truly realistic and mutually satisfactory. If there's doubt about whether a solution meets those two criteria, you'll want to discuss possible modifications to the original idea or consider alternatives until you and your child agree on a solution that comes closer to the mark. By the way, notice that you're not brainstorming dozens of solutions before you start evaluating each one; that can become overwhelming. Better to consider one solution at a time; if the first one isn't realistic and mutually satisfactory, either refine it or consider another until one comes closer to the mark.

Missing Ingredients: Skipping Steps
· · · · ·

Each of the three ingredients, each step, is indispensable in the collaborative resolution of a problem. If you skip a step, you're leaving out an important ingredient, and that's not a recipe for success.

If you skip the Empathy step, you won't know your child's concerns, and whatever solution you come up with won't address those concerns. Those solutions tend not to work very well. If that sounds a lot like Plan A, you may be on to something:

Parent: I want you to do your homework before hockey practice from now on, because if you don't do your homework before hockey practice, you end up staying up really late to finish it and then you're tired for school the next day. How can we work that out?

Kid: Sounds like you've already worked it out.

If you skip the Define-Adult-Concerns step—this is where you're entering your concerns into consideration—then your concerns won't get addressed:

Parent: I've noticed that you've been staying up really late to get your homework done on the days you have hockey practice. What's up?

Kid: I need a break when I get home from school, so I don't want to do my homework before hockey practice. So I end up staying up really late to finish it.

Parent: OK.

But as you read in chapter 5, it's often the case that adults enter a solution rather than a concern in this step, causing Plan B to revert to Plan A. Let's see what that might sound like:

Parent: I've noticed that you've been staying up really late to get your homework done on the days you have hockey practice. What's up?

Kid: I need a break when I get home from school, so I don't want to do my homework before hockey practice. So I end up staying up really late to finish it.

Parent: So you're really tired when you get home from school and you don't want to do your homework before hockey practice.

Kid: Sometimes I'm too tired to do it after hockey practice, so I have to get up really early the next morning to do it. And sometimes I'm too tired in the morning too, so then I try to get it done during my free period.

Parent (entering a solution rather than a concern): Well, I don't want you staying up that late and I don't want you getting up that early. So you really need to do the homework before hockey.

Kid: I don't want to do it before hockey! I'm tired when I get home from school and I need some time to chill!

If you skip the Invitation step, this simply means that you've waited two steps before reverting back to Plan A. If you do this, your kid will lose interest in participating in the first two steps of Plan B.

Parent: I've noticed that you've been staying up really late to get your homework done on the days you have hockey practice. What's up?

Kid: I need a break when I get home from school, so I don't want to do my homework before hockey practice. So I end up staying up really late to finish it.

Parent: So you're really tired when you get home from school and you don't want to do your homework before hockey practice.

Kid: Sometimes I'm too tired to do it after hockey practice, so I have to get up really early the next morning to do it. And sometimes I'm too tired in the morning too, so then I try to get it done during my free period.

Parent (entering a concern): Well, my concern is that I don't want you to be tired at school the next day. This is an important year for you, and I want to make sure you're at your best.

Kid: OK.

Parent (skipping the invitation and heading straight into a unilateral solution): So I've decided that you're not going to hockey practice if the homework isn't done.

Kid: What?!

Parent (using one of the classic rationales for Plan A): I'm doing this for your own good.

Kid: Well, that's a dumb idea and I'm not doing it!

Parent: Watch your tone, young man . . .

Q & A

Question: How will I know when I'm ready to do my first Plan B?

Answer: If you've never done Plan B, you may never feel completely ready. But it's good to get the first one out of the way. Then keep practicing.

Question: My first Plan B was a disaster. What went wrong?

Answer: Trying to partner with your kid on solving a problem is never a disaster. If it didn't go as well as you hoped, you might want to reread this chapter and chapter 5 to figure out why. But if in the Empathy step you gathered some new information about your child's concerns on a given unsolved problem, you did well. If you didn't finish the Empathy step, that's OK; there's always tomorrow. You also did well if in the Define-Adult-Concerns step you resisted the temptation to impose solutions and instead were able to identify your own concerns. If you made it to the Invitation and were able to collaborate with your child on a realistic and mutually satisfactory solution, that's great. Hopefully, the solution you and your child agreed upon will stand the test of time. If it doesn't, you'll find out soon enough, and then it's back to Plan B to figure out why and to come up with a solution that is more realistic or mutually satisfactory than the first one, or one that addresses concerns that may not have been identified in your first try. When you think the time is right, move on to another unsolved problem. Even if your child refused to participate, you probably picked up some brownie points for trying. Maybe she'll be more receptive next time.

Question: What if the first solution doesn't work?

Answer: In The Real World, the first solution often doesn't get the job done. In The Real World, durable solutions come after the ones that didn't work so well. The important thing is to learn from the ones that didn't work so well so subsequent solutions are more likely to succeed.

It may be tempting to blame the kid for solutions that don't work. Remember, the kid isn't the only one who signed off on the solution.

Question: What if my child and I agree on a solution and then she won't do what she agreed to? Should I punish her?

Answer: You wouldn't want to punish her for a solution that you *both* agreed to. If your kid isn't following through on a solution that she (and you) agreed to, that's usually a sign that the solution wasn't as realistic and mutually satisfactory as it may first have seemed. That's not a failure, just a reminder that the first solution to a problem often doesn't get the job done. If one or both of the two parties can't execute their part of the solution, go back to Plan B to come up with a solution that's more realistic. If the concerns of one or both parties weren't satisfactorily addressed by the solution, go back to Plan B to come up with a solution that does address the concerns of both parties. By the way, the original solution can only address the concerns that were actually verbalized in the first two steps, but it wouldn't address the concerns that *weren't* verbalized. Go back to Plan B to see if there were concerns that weren't verbalized. Punishment isn't going to increase the likelihood of your child following through on a solution that isn't realistic and mutually satisfactory, nor is it going to increase the likelihood that your child will participate in Plan B again.

Question: Should I expect 100 percent adherence to a solution? If I'm not getting 100 percent, does that mean it wasn't realistic or just that the child needs help accomplishing it?

Answer: I'm not sure anyone is 100 percent reliable on solutions. But you are expecting that the problem the solution is addressing will be largely solved. If it's not, returning to Plan B will help you figure out why and refine the solution.

Question: Do I need to enforce solutions?
Answer: You're conflating your role in Plan A with your role in Plan B. With Plan B, you and your child are both devoted to the solution and are equally committed to its success in solving a problem, so you're out of the business of enforcing solutions that you've imposed.

Question: I've been making my child apologize when she does something wrong. Is this really accomplishing anything?
Answer: Forced apologies probably don't accomplish much. Plus, you're probably making your child apologize for her *behavior*, and you really want to be more focused on collaborating with your child to solve the *problems* that are causing that behavior. Apologies don't solve problems.

Question: Would you say the same about having my child make amends for her behavior?
Answer: It's possible that engaging your kid in a discussion about how to make amends might be productive in helping her think about how her behavior has been hurtful to another person. But as with apologies, making amends won't solve the problem that caused the hurtful behavior, so solving that problem is still paramount.

Question: In the story at the end of the last chapter, it seemed like the solution required that the child remember to do a lot of new things. What if she has difficulty remembering to do them all the time? Can I remind her sometimes?

Answer: If you think your child can reliably perform solutions you've agreed upon but may have difficulty remembering them, incorporating reminders into the solution could make very good sense. If the reminding turns into nagging, then the solution probably wasn't realistic and would need to be revisited.

Question: It's hard to decide which Plan to use on the spur of the moment. What am I doing wrong?

Answer: Well, you shouldn't be making that decision on the spur of the moment most of the time anyway. You should be deciding what problems you're trying to solve—and what problems you're not trying to solve just yet—ahead of time. Then you won't have to be so quick on your feet.

Question: Yes, but is it possible to use Plan B if a problem pops up? What would that sound like?

Answer: On the rare occasions in which that might happen, yes, it's possible to use Plan B in the heat of the moment. You just don't want to make a habit of it. Emergency Plan B differs from Proactive Plan B primarily in the timing and the wording of the Empathy step. The Empathy step of Emergency Plan B wouldn't begin with an introduction (as in Proactive Plan B), because it's already too late to be proactive. So you'd head straight into reflective listening. Here are a few examples of what that would sound like:

Kid: I'm not going to hockey practice today.
Parent: You're not going to hockey practice today. What's up?

Kid: I'm not going to school today. I need a mental health day.
Parent: You're not going to school today. What's up?

Kid: I can't do this homework!
Parent: You can't do the homework. What's up?

Then, of course, you'd want to come to the clearest possible understanding of your child's concern, perspective, or point of view. After that, you'd continue on to the other two steps.

Question: So if I don't make it through all three steps of Plan B in the first attempt, that's OK?
Answer: Absolutely. You never know how much information you're going to gather in the Empathy step, so you never know how long it's going to take before you move on to the next steps. Solving problems collaboratively is a process, and one with no stopwatch.

Question: I started using Plan B with my daughter, and she talked! In fact, she talked so much that I started becoming overwhelmed with all the information I was getting and all the problems we need to solve. Now what?
Answer: It's true, sometimes Plan B opens the information floodgates, and you find out there were even more problems to solve than those you identified on your initial list. While that can feel overwhelming, your awareness of all of those additional unsolved problems is a good thing. Your goal is to

add the new unsolved problems to your list, perhaps repri-oritize, and continue the mission of solving one problem at a time. If you find that your kid is providing an enormous amount of information in the Empathy step, ask your child if it's OK if you write things down; you don't want to forget a thing.

Question: It sounds like I should get "Because I said so" out of my vocabulary. Yes?

Answer: That expression certainly isn't going to help you partner with your child on durable, mutually satisfactory solutions to the problems that are affecting her life.

Question: But I can still set limits?

Answer: Remember, you're setting limits by having expecta-tions and by being devoted to having your child meet them. If, for example, you expect your child to eat dinner with the family (and not in front of the TV), keep her room reasonably clean, get to bed at a reasonable hour, get home in time for curfew, work hard in school, get to school on time, and not drive under the influence of drugs or alcohol, then you're set-ting limits.

But if your child isn't meeting an expectation, you have an unsolved problem. *At that point, "limit setting" and "problem-solving" become synonymous.* As you know, if you solve that problem using Plan A, you're not only solving the problem unilaterally, you're also slamming the door on understand-ing and addressing your kid's concerns, increasing the likelihood of adversarial interactions, pressing ahead with uninformed solutions, and probably not solving the problem durably. When you solve problems using Plan B, you learn about what's getting in your child's way, decrease adversarial interactions, work together on solutions that are realistic and mutually satisfactory, and solve problems durably. You're setting limits either way. It's just that one way is a whole lot more effective and conducive to a partnership than the other.

Question: I've been having my kid sign contracts—you know, where I specify my expectations and my kid agrees to meet them and gets rewards if she does. Not good?

Answer: It's a pretty safe bet that your child is already clear about your expectations, so you probably don't need contracts for that. And if your child is having difficulty meeting certain expectations, it's a safe bet that something is getting in the way, and a contract and those rewards won't help you figure that out or resolve it. So you still have information to gather and problems to solve, and contracts won't help you accomplish those two things.

Question: Isn't Plan B passive?

Answer: Plan B isn't passive at all. It's a *very* active approach to parenting. Many adults believe that "active" means being harsh and punitive. Now you know better. Some parents also view Plan B as a show of weakness and adult-imposed consequences as a sign of strength. But collaborating with your kid on solving the problems that affect her life isn't about strength or weakness; it's about what works.

Question: But does Plan B make it clear to my child that I disapprove of some of her actions?

Answer: Absolutely. You'll be talking with her about your concerns about the actions of which you disapprove in the Define-Adult-Concerns step. And you'll be getting your concerns addressed in the Invitation. But it's also good to remember that her actions (her *behaviors*) are probably the by-product of specific unsolved problems, and those problems (not her behaviors) are going to be the focal point of Plan B.

Question: If I'm always collaborating with my child, and always reaching a solution that is agreeable to both of us, isn't there the potential that she'll learn that she only has to comply with my expectations if she feels like it? In The Real World, she will have to do things that she may not necessarily feel like doing.

Answer: Your child is already meeting expectations that she doesn't feel like meeting. She may not always feel like doing her homework (but perhaps does it anyway), may not always feel like studying for a test (but perhaps is doing that too), and may not always love what you made for dinner (but may be eating it anyway). You're collaborating with your child on the expectations she's having *difficulty* meeting.

Question: What if she actually says, "Because I don't feel like it," when I raise a concern with her?

Answer: Start drilling so as to better understand what she means. Then collaborate on solutions to address her concerns.

Question: So Plan B isn't just a clever way to get my kid to do what I want?

Answer: That's right. There's nothing clever about Plan B. It's just the hard work of solving problems collaboratively.

Question: I have this feeling my kid is going to see through what I'm trying to do when I'm solving problems collaboratively with her.

Answer: Excellent! Because solving problems collaboratively is a transparent process. Plan B isn't a technique aimed at tricking your kid into doing things your way. If your kid knows that you're deeply invested in understanding and clarifying her concern, perspective, or point of view on a given unsolved problem, and she understands your concern or perspective, and you two are working together toward solutions that are realistic and mutually satisfactory, then there's nothing to "see through."

Question: Is Plan B the only means through which I would gather information from my child about her concern, perspective, or point of view on a particular issue?

Answer: You can *informally* talk with your child and listen to her point of view on lots of different topics besides unsolved problems whenever you like. And presumably you've been offering your point of view on many of those topics as well, without imposing your will, insisting that your child adopt your point of view, or being dismissive or judgmental about her point of view.

Question: You don't think Plan A is a good way to build character and promote grit?

Answer: If you're referring to a child's ability to get back up when she gets knocked down (by a problem) in life, I'm not exactly sure how Plan A would help. I'm quite clear about how Plan B would help. Your kid doesn't need you to be the one knocking her down; life will take care of that. Your kid needs you to help her learn how to get back up. And, as you've read, there are some additional characteristics you badly want to foster in your child—empathy, taking into account how one's behavior is affecting other people, honesty, taking another person's perspective, and resolving disagreements in ways that do not involve conflict—but Plan A doesn't foster those characteristics. Plan B does. Again, more on that in chapter 9.

Question: Can you say more about Assumption-Free Living?
Answer: Sure. It's an effort to notice when you're making an assumption about your kid and get rid of it—*fast*. As you've read, parents are renowned for being quite sure they know what's going on with their kid and forming solutions based on those assumptions. Of course, if the assumptions are off base, the solutions those assumptions give rise to will miss the mark as well. When you can forgo those assumptions, you're free to find out what's really going on with your kid. The nice thing about Plan B is that it provides you with another option besides assuming: *asking*.

· · · · ·

Denise had arranged an appointment with Hank to continue their very abbreviated discussion. She decided to limit the discussion to his difficulties getting along with his sister (rather than including his difficulties with Nick in the same discussion). She strategically planted Nick and Charlotte in front of the TV set and sat down with Hank at the kitchen table. "I know you don't want to do this," Denise began, with Hank looking completely disinterested.

"Then why are you making me?" said Hank.

"Well, I'm not exactly making you. But I don't like the way people are treating each other around here sometimes and I need your help in making it better."

Hank rolled his eyes.

"So can we talk a little about the difficulty you're having getting along with your sister?"

"How come you're not talking to her about it?"

"I will be talking to her about it," said Denise. "But I thought I'd get your take on things first."

"I already told you my take on things. She's annoying."

"Yes, I remember that part," said Denise. "But I didn't really get much more than that."

Hank sighed. "She's always coming into my room without permission. She has her own bedroom and I have to share mine with Igmo," said Hank, using the disparaging nickname he'd coined for his younger brother. "I'm the oldest. How come the brat gets her own bedroom?"

Denise was tempted to answer Hank's question for the 127th time but decided to continue drilling for information. "So she's always coming into your room without permission. And she has her own bedroom and you think you should have your own bedroom because you're the oldest."

"Right."

"Any other reasons you're having difficulty getting along with her?"

"She always has her stupid TV shows on and she goes nuts if I want to watch something I like. And she knows you'll take her side if she screams about it."

"Hank, do you mind if I write some of this stuff down?" asked Denise.

"I mean, I think I already knew about most of this stuff, but I don't want to forget anything."

"You do know about all this stuff! But you don't do anything! That's why there's no point in talking about it."

"Well, I have tried to do some things, but what I've tried to do hasn't worked. I haven't helped you guys solve these problems. I think I didn't know how. But I want you to give me another chance. You're not happy with the way things are—that's pretty clear. And I'm not happy. I don't think Nick and Charlotte are happy either. So I don't think there's much choice but for us to try even harder to solve them."

"Well, since you haven't done anything, I have to," said Hank.

"What do you mean?"

"If they bug me, I bug them back. And I bug them back way worse."

"Yes, I understand that's been your strategy. And now I understand how you got to that point. But I don't think that strategy is working. It just makes everyone bug each other more."

"Survival of the fittest," said Hank, using one of his favorite lines.

"I think there's a better way," said Denise. "Can we keep talking about how Charlotte is bugging you?"

"We've covered it," said Hank.

"So if we solve these problems, you feel like you could get along better with Charlotte?"

"No promises," said Hank. "But I don't think you can solve them anyways."

"See, that's the thing. We were all thinking that *I'm* the one who's supposed to solve these problems. But that's just turned me into a referee. And I hate being a referee. Plus, I'm not very good at it. I have to help you guys solve these problems with each other. I can help you solve them, but I can't do it on my own. I need your help."

"What about Charlotte?"

"I'm going to need Charlotte's help too. I'm talking to you about it first. But let me make sure I have my list straight. She comes into your room without asking. That's one problem that we need to solve. And you think you should have your own bedroom since you're the oldest. That's another. And she's always watching her shows on TV so you don't get to watch the shows you like. Do I have it?"

"Yup," grumbled Hank.

"Which one should we solve first?"

"None. This is pointless."

"Yeah, maybe, but which one do you want to start working on first?"

"The TV."

"So tell me a little more about that one," said Denise, returning to the Empathy step for that specific unsolved problem.

"She has, like, unlimited TV. And she watches really dumb shows that I don't want to watch. And she knows you'll take her side, so I almost never get to watch the shows I want unless she's, like, in bed or at a friend's house or something."

"Got it. So your concern is that you almost never get to watch the shows you want because Charlotte has a monopoly on the TV set and I always take her side."

"Yes."

"Do you want to hear my concern?"

"If I have to."

"My concern is that you kind of bully her when you want to watch something on TV."

"I wouldn't if you'd stop taking her side!"

"Let me finish, please. I know that's your view. I can't let you bully your younger sister. You're bigger than her, sometimes you hurt her, and it's just not fair for you to throw your weight around like that. It makes her feel bad. Do you understand?"

"Whatever."

"So what we're going to try to do is come up with a solution that addresses my concern—I can't let you treat your sister in ways that make her feel bad—and your concern, which is that you want to be able to watch shows you like on TV."

"So what's the solution?" asked Hank.

"I have no idea," said Denise. "I need to talk to Charlotte next to find out what her concerns are. Then we're going to get together—me, you, and her—and we're going to come up with a solution that works for all of us. Not me . . . *we*."

"We done?"

"We're done for now."

You can use Plan B to solve problems between two kids and not just between a kid and an adult? Yes, you can. But as you just read, it might look a little like "shuttle diplomacy" in the beginning, as it may be best to gather the concerns of both kids before putting them together to solve the problem. It's good, also, to take yourself out of the role of referee; it's better for the kids to realize that you're the Problem-Solving Facilitator, not the solution machine.

. . . . .

Dan was awakened in the middle of the night by the sense that Kristin was no longer in the bed with him. He reached over for confirmation. Kristin was definitely not in the bed. As he tried to get his bearings, he thought he noticed Kristin pacing in the dark.

"Kristin?"

"Yeah."

"What are you doing?"

"Pacing."

Dan propped himself up on a pillow. "Why are you pacing?"

"Can't sleep."

"Because of Taylor?" This was a safe bet, as Taylor was Kristin's foremost preoccupation.

"Yes, Taylor," Kristin confirmed.

"Come back to bed. You can't let her eat you up like this."

"Well, I can't help it."

"What are you thinking about?"

"Everything."

"What's everything?"

"It doesn't help to talk about it."

"Come on—tell me," Dan prodded, patting the bed so Kristin would sit down.

"She doesn't get enough sleep. I know she hasn't started her term paper in literature yet. She's not studying enough for the SATs. I don't know where she is half the time. I want her to get into a good college. I want her to be happy. I want to get along with her." Kristin dolefully sat down on the bed.

"I know."

"Did you think about David and Julie this much?" Kristin asked, referring to Dan's kids from his first marriage.

Dan tried to choose his words carefully, despite being half-asleep. "Um, sometimes. But not really as much as you think about Taylor."

"So what's the matter with me?"

"You care about her a lot. But I think there's such a thing as caring too much. You can't care about her so much that you drive yourself crazy. She's OK. She's just spreading her wings a little. Kinda what she's supposed to be doing at this age."

"I know it's what she's supposed to be doing. I just think she started doing it a lot earlier than most kids. It's hard for me. I'm a control freak."

"You do like things to be 'just so,'" Dan said. "It's just that Taylor isn't a 'just so' kid. She's Taylor. And Taylor is going to be Taylor."

"Yeah, well, that doesn't mean she shouldn't answer her cell phone when I call."

"I think we need to try approaching her differently about that," said Dan, strategically using the word *we* instead of *you* to see if that might make it easier to hear. It didn't work.

"You mean *me*, right?" was Kristin's response. "She *loves* you. You never say no."

"I actually meant *we*," said Dan. "It would be good if we were on the same page."

"Well, you won't get on *my* page, so we should be clear about whose page we're talking about."

"Is this something we can talk about without it turning into a fight?" Dan asked.

"Fine, let's do it your way. Let's let her walk all over me."

"I don't think you should let her walk all over you. It only feels like she walks all over you because you draw a line in the sand that you can't possibly uphold. In my business, that's called saber rattling. And any good attorney is going to call my bluff. I don't think you should take all-or-nothing stands with her. It just makes her take all-or-nothing stands with you."

"I don't know what to do instead."

Dan pondered this. "A long time ago, we had some difficulties with Julie," he said, referring to his older daughter. "We saw a therapist a few times. And she taught us how to solve problems with her in a way that didn't cause conflict."

"Good luck getting Taylor to go to a therapist!" Kristin scoffed. "And do you know how many parenting books I've read?"

"I'm not saying we need to go to a therapist. I just think I learned some things in dealing with Julie that could be helpful with Taylor. Come to think of it, I'm probably still applying to Taylor what I learned with Julie without even realizing it."

Kristin wasn't buying it. "I'm not going to have her walk all over me."

"It's not about letting her walk all over you. It's about how parents talk to kids. And how we listen to them. And solve problems together."

Kristin seemed to be tiring of the conversation. "I'm tired of hearing about everything I'm doing wrong with Taylor and everything you did right with Julie and that Taylor's problems are all my fault."

Kristin climbed back into bed. Dan was glad to see that the dead-of-night conversation seemed to be ending. But he couldn't resist replying. "Taylor's problems aren't all your fault. And they're *our* problems, not *her* problems. I think we need to start working on them together."

Of course we worry about our kids. They're our *kids*. And of course different parents are more stressed by unsolved problems than others. If you're thinking we should consider those realities a bit further, you need only turn the page.

Chapter 7

PARENTAL ANGST

In the first few chapters of this book, we considered your role in your kid's life and your options in trying to fulfill that role, with an emphasis on your role as partner. Then you read a lot about how to solve problems collaboratively, and in the last chapter, you learned about the potential difficulties involved in doing so. Now we're going to talk about you a little more, because this chapter is about one of the greatest impediments to the partnership you're trying to create with your child: *your anxiety*.

It's good that you're taking your job as a parent seriously and that you're concerned about your kid's outcome. And it's also good that you don't want your kid to make the same mistakes you did, or do irreparable harm to himself or his future. But if your anxiety gets the better of you, it can blind you. It can make it hard to see the forest for the trees. It can cause you to hold on too tight or push too hard. It can make you see red, make you overreact. It can cloud your judgment and cause you to respond more urgently than is necessary. It can prompt you to take the express bus back to the Dictatorial Kingdom.

What's making you anxious?

- Feeling that your kid isn't turning out OK, isn't making the most of his opportunities, or is having trouble meeting more than his share of expectations.
- Feeling embarrassed by your kid or that the expectations he's having difficulty meeting reflect poorly on you and your parenting.
- Feeling that, despite your best efforts, things aren't getting better.

Because you have a lot riding on that kid, it's easy to have your outlook on life heavily influenced—too heavily—by how your kid is doing. His high school investment club came in first place in the state? You're floating on air. He flunked his math test in the seventh grade? Disaster. He'll never get into college! Not a good one anyway. He doesn't have proper study habits at the age of six? Catastrophe. Better get that squared away now, or it's going to be ugly when he's eighteen!

But as we've already established, your parenting isn't the sole determining factor in what your child does and how well he does it. Given that you're not the only influence in your child's life, and that your gene pool can express itself in highly disparate ways, that kid of yours is a reflection of a lot of things—again, a *symphony* of factors—many of which are not necessarily your doing and are not totally (or even sort of) within your control. For some parents, that diffusion of responsibility is a relief. For others—perhaps those who operate under the illusion of complete and total control and feel that if they just blow their horn hard enough, they'll be heard above the din—it only produces more anxiety.

It's certainly your role to exert some influence when your child is heading in a direction that causes you or other adults concern. And now you know how to do that. But, especially when those unmet expectations make you feel like an inadequate parent, or when you're worried that your kid isn't turning out OK, or when he's struggling to meet a lot of expectations, or when you're feeling embarrassed when things aren't getting better rapidly, it's tempting to go overboard in the influence department, to feel that setting him back on the right course, firmly and decisively, needs to occur *right now!* And that's when a lot of parents blaze a trail back to Plan A.

We humans—parents included—tend to become the most anxious when we feel powerless: powerless to achieve certain desired outcomes, powerless to effect desired changes. Feeling powerless often causes us to apply more power. Yet often the more power we apply, the more powerless we feel.

But you're not powerless as a parent. You have a very powerful tool to help you: Plan B. The knowledge that you can influence your kid without the use of power is very . . . well, powerful. It's going to help you tone things down in your own head, help you maintain your perspective. It's going to help you keep your balance.

What balance? The balance between your kid's skills, preferences, beliefs, values, personality traits, goals, and direction and your experience, wisdom, and values. Maintaining that balance isn't a perfect art. It's hard. But hard is preferable to powerless.

Maintaining your perspective is crucial to keeping your anxiety under control. Here are some reminders that might help:

- Your child needs the freedom to try his emerging identity on for size without feeling like it's an unmitigated disaster if he needs to refine things a little or take a mulligan. You're being a good parent when you allow that to happen. If you're overreacting or holding on too tight, he won't have room to grow.

- Your child also needs the space to make mistakes and learn from them. You're being a good parent when you let that happen too. If you're trying too hard to control the outcome or being too judgmental when he trips over his own feet, he'll be overly concerned about making mistakes and won't have the chance to learn from them.

- Your child also needs the opportunity to right the ship on his own when he runs into troubled waters. And he needs you to watch closely to see how he's doing. If you're not watching closely enough, he could tire of floundering and give up. If you throw him the life vest at the first sign of floundering, he'll never learn to swim. If he's able to right the ship often enough, you'll start to have faith in his ability to do so. He may actually have a pretty decent ship-righting track record and—though your memories of the times when he didn't handle troubled waters quite so well may be more poignant—it's good to reflect on that.

- Your child needs you to know how to help him right the ship if he can't do it on his own. That's Plan B. If you rely too heavily on Plan A to right the ship, you won't have a Problem-Solving Partner; you'll just have a lot of conflict.

But isn't it normal for kids and parents to fight with each other?

If "normal" means the *norm*, then perhaps yes is the answer. If "normal" means *necessary*, then no. Conflict between you and your child isn't a given; it isn't inevitable. *Your relationship with your child isn't destined to be adversarial.* The recipe for parent-child conflict is now familiar to you:

- Pour unmet expectations into a pot.
- Stir in the failure to identify concerns.
- Add competing solutions (power struggles) to the mix.
- Season to taste with a dash (or more) of parental anxiety.
- Bring to a boil with imposed solutions (Plan A).

But if you're solving problems collaboratively, you're changing the recipe. By the way, a *dash* of parental anxiety is probably a good thing; it'll keep you on your toes and alert you to problems that need to be solved. It's anxiety *overflow* that will cause you to lose perspective and respond in ways that are counterproductive. A little parental frustration is a good thing as well. Your frustration also signals that there's an expectation your child is having difficulty meeting and that you need information about whatever is making it hard for him to meet that expectation. Too much frustration, though, and you'll overreact. By the way, there are some parents who respond to high levels of anxiety and frustration over their children's unmet expectations by reacting in the opposite direction: they eventually stop caring about and trying to solve problems altogether. This, of course, can be as counterproductive as overreacting. *In the same way that your child's behavior communicates that there's a problem that needs to be solved, your anxiety and frustration signal the exact same thing.*

When I was a new parent, I tended to become extremely anxious if one of my kids—my firstborn in particular—ran a fever. *What if there's something terribly wrong? Aren't I being negligent if I don't bring her to the pediatrician immediately? Isn't that what a good par-*

ent would do? How am I going to feel if I delay and there's something really serious going on? So, duly alarmed, I'd rush her—with not a moment to spare, really—to the pediatrician. I was always greatly relieved to learn that there were several different bugs going around, that my daughter's symptoms fit the profile of at least one of them, and that she'd probably be fine in one to three days. With my anxiety now reduced, I could focus on giving my daughter the empathy and care she needed. Over time, I learned a few things. First, I could probably ease up on the Tylenol. Fever is a good thing, a sign that my daughter's immune system had mobilized to fight an infection and was pretty darn good at it. The fever would eventually lift; the vomiting would end; she'd be OK. If it had ever turned out that my daughter couldn't fight an infection on her own, or something was seriously the matter, I was watching closely and would have made sure she received the additional care she needed. Perhaps most important, *I learned that showing that I cared wasn't necessarily best expressed by taking control or overdoing it on intervention.*

It's no different with other aspects of your child's development. What are some of the telltale signs that your anxiety is over the top?

- if you can't stop thinking about your kid and how he's doing and the problems that might be in his path
- if you're losing sleep over fairly mundane problems of development
- if you're screaming a lot
- if you find yourself overcorrecting, overdirecting, overcoaching, and overcriticizing so that things will turn out fine
- if you can't stop asking your child about every detail of his existence

How will the approach described in this book help you keep your perspective?

- First, it provides you with new lenses: *kids do well if they can—if your kid could do well, he would do well, because doing well is preferable*. When you feel overwhelmed with anxiety or tempted to impose a solution on your kid, this is a worthy mantra.

- Second, it provides you with a new game plan. You're going to identify and prioritize unsolved problems ahead of time, so you're not trying to solve them all at once and you're not trying to solve them emergently, in the heat of the moment. When you have a concrete, proactive approach, you'll feel less overwhelmed.

- Third, when you start experiencing some success with Plan B, then unmet expectations aren't going to freak you out anymore because you'll have faith that you and your kid can deal with them. Together. Plan A isn't going to give you that faith. With Plan A, you're flying solo, and the problems still aren't solved. With Plan B, the pressure is off. You don't have to come up with solutions on your own. You have a teammate.

- Plan B is also going to ensure that you gather information from your child so you're clear about his concerns and about what's getting in his way. And he'll know what yours are too. His voice will be heard. Your voice will be heard. When your child engages in the problem-solving process with you, you'll be reassured that he is resilient and capable.

- Plan B also relieves you of the pressure to establish who's right and who's wrong. Rather than ruminating about what solution or consequences you should impose, and dreading a big fight or the effort required to force your kid to comply, you will be partnering with your kid on solutions that are realistic and mutually satisfactory. Rather than continuously bumping up against each other, you and your kid will be working together.

- When you're not bumping up against your kid, you start to have the freedom to learn about his skills, preferences, beliefs, values, personality traits, goals, and direction. You may be impressed with what you learn about him, even if it's not what you'd planned on. And when he's not bumping up against you, he has the freedom to learn about your experience, wisdom, and values. You'll be able to impart those to him, and doing so will let your mind rest easier.

- Your new approach should slow things down for you and help you achieve a level of detachment and perspective. If you and your kid can get into a Plan B rhythm, you'll start feeling less pressure to intervene *right now!* You'll come to recognize that usually there's less to worry about than you may have thought and that you have more time than it may have seemed.

- The new approach is also going to help you stay focused on your goals as a parent. You're trying to help your child figure out who he is and have influence at the same time. You're trying to communicate well. You're trying to have a good relationship. And you're trying to raise a human being, to foster the human characteristics that are most admirable, not the ones that bring out the less desirable side of both of you.

- Your new approach is also going to help you stay away from counterproductive communication patterns that make it extremely difficult for you and your child to hear and clarify each other's concerns and that increase the likelihood of conflict. Here are just a few of them:

Mind Reading: This is where parents and kids infer each other's motives or thoughts:

Kristin: The reason Taylor doesn't tell us where she is or answer her cell phone is because she's doing things she doesn't want us to know about.

It's fairly common for people to make inferences about one another. The problem is that we're *wrong* a meaningful percentage of the time. The other problem is that we don't *think* we're wrong a meaningful percentage of the time, so we respond to our kids based on inference rather than information. The Empathy step of Plan B is a much more productive way to find out what your kid is *actually* thinking. You'll probably never be a great mind reader, but with a little practice, you can become highly skilled at the Empathy step.

Adults are not the only ones who may rely too heavily on inference; after a while, kids jump into the fray:

Taylor: The reason you call my cell phone so much is because you want to control my life.

Your child's prospects for excelling at mind reading aren't great either. There's a much better way for him to know what your concerns are: the Define-Adult-Concerns step.

Catastrophizing: This is where parents greatly exaggerate the effect of current behavior on a child's future well being.

Kristin: Fine, don't answer your cell phone. Ruin your life. If you want to screw up your chances of getting into a good college, that's your choice.

Often parents—especially those who feel that their concerns aren't being heard—blow their concerns out of proportion in the misguided belief that doing so will get the message through. But as you've read, kids who have their concerns heard, validated, and addressed tend to be far more willing to take others' concerns into account. So you won't need to blow things out of proportion to be heard. And if you and your kid are collaborative partners, your concerns will be addressed.

Interrupting: Often parents feel so uncertain that their concerns will be heard and addressed that they make it almost impossible for a kid to voice his own concerns. Interrupting begets interrupting; raised voices beget raised voices. But when you're using Plan B, you know your concerns will be heard and addressed. It just takes some practice to start to feel a sense of assurance about it.

One of the nice things about Plan B is that it structures the flow of information and the process of problem-solving. Adult concerns aren't discussed in the Empathy step. Kids' concerns aren't discussed in the Define-Adult-Concerns step. The concerns of both parties are of equal legitimacy, so there's no need for one party to talk over the other. All concerns will be heard, so there's no need to interrupt.

Are you still going to be anxious about your child falling down, about your child being in danger? Yes—there's no question. When my own kids were quite young, I felt I needed to be hypervigilant in order to make sure they didn't injure themselves. It was exhausting. And even with all my vigilance, I couldn't protect them all the time. Case in point: my daughter, age three. I had always let her stand on a step stool so she could help me make scrambled eggs at the stove, and she'd learned that the electric burner was hot when it was orange. So it didn't occur to her that the burner I'd turned off a few minutes earlier—and that was no longer orange but had gone back to black—was still quite hot. So, when my back was turned one day, she touched it. She didn't stop screaming for hours. Did the episode scar her for life? Hard to say for sure, but apparently not. She actually doesn't remember it. (By the way, there's another burned-hand story involving my son and the oven, but I'm not allowed to tell it in this book because it occurred on the watch of his paternal grandmother.)

I don't worry about burns or broken bones so much anymore. Now that my kids are fifteen and eighteen years old, there are different aspects of their lives that have grabbed my attention and concern. We'll talk more about that in the next chapter.

Is your kid going to embarrass you sometimes? Sure. It may help to remember that you've embarrassed yourself a few times over the years and that when you did, hopefully you learned from the experience, brushed yourself off, and got on with it. Try not to worry about what other parents or the neighbors or your extended family is going to think. Try not to compare yourself to them or their children. Allowing yourself to be overcome with embarrassment or worry about what they think will only cloud your ability to see your kid for who he is. As a parent, your primary focus is on your kid's development, and development doesn't occur in a straight line. There are bumps in the road, and much as we may be tempted to steer our child away from them, the bumps are good.

And by the way, when it comes to being embarrassed, you don't have a corner on the market. By the time your kid hits early adolescence, he will be the one who's embarrassed by you.

It's worth noting here that Plan B can't do it all. You'll also need the perspective of knowing what unsolved problems are likely to crop up at various points in development and knowing which ones are cause for greater alarm than others. Again, we'll cover that in greater detail in the next chapter.

Q & A

Question: Don't you think my kid needs me to just take control sometimes?

Answer: Sometimes, perhaps. But those times should be rare.

Question: So Plan A isn't the only way to make sure my kid turns out OK?

Answer: There's no way to ensure that your kid turns out OK. There are only ways to *improve his odds* of turning out OK. Plan A might reduce your anxiety temporarily—make you feel like you're actually doing something decisive—but it's not going to make you feel less anxious over the long haul, because it places all the responsibility for your child doing well on *you*. You'll start becoming less anxious when you give your kid the chance to prove that if he falls, he can get back up again, often without your help.

Question: I have very clear ideas about the way things should be and I like things to turn out "just right" for my kid. My spouse says my parenting suffers from the "curse of certainty." Any words of wisdom?

Answer: Well, we might expect a higher potential for incompatibility between you and your child, since his ideas about the way things should be and his definition of "just right" are likely to be different from yours, at least in some realms of life. The reality is that the process of raising kids is filled with uncertainties. You can't know or control the outcome. The best you can do is parent in a way that balances your desire for influence with your child's characteristics; in other words, to be responsive to the hand you've been dealt. That's as close to "just right" as you're likely to come.

Question: I don't know if I can stay unemotional when I'm talking to my child about things I care a lot about.

Answer: You may be right. Some problems can be pretty emotional to talk about. Your kid may be OK with your being a little emotional—and may even interpret the emotion as a sign of caring—but may have less tolerance for emotional *overflow*. So maybe you want to try hard not to overdo it, knowing that the more emotion you express, the harder it is for your kid to participate in the process. But it's also the case that a lot of the pent-up emotion parents express is due to the fact that they haven't had a mechanism for reliably having their concerns addressed, so the concerns are expressed more powerfully than is necessary. As you and your kid come to recognize that Plan B provides that mechanism—and as you both experience some success in solving problems—those discussions are likely to become a lot less emotional.

Question: It's not just parental anxiety that's making it hard for me to do Plan B. It's time, or the lack of it. Between work, and school, and baseball and lacrosse practice, and piano lessons, and homework, and different schedules for different kids, when exactly are we supposed to do Plan B?

Answer: All those activities are wonderful, but finding the time to solve problems with your kid is more important. You need to commit to carving out the time. Plus, you don't always have to arrange a formal time to solve problems collaboratively with your child; it can be done on the way to baseball practice, at bedtime, when you're doing the dishes together after dinner . . . whenever. Otherwise, you're basically saying that you don't have time to help your kid solve the problems that affect his life. And we know that's not what you want. Plus, as you know, dealing with the same unsolved problems on a daily basis takes far longer than taking the time to solve them.

Question: Why am I prioritizing problem-solving? Colleges don't care about how my kid solves problems. They care about grades and SAT scores and extracurricular activities.

Answer: Colleges certainly do care about grades and SAT scores and extracurriculars. But a lot of colleges and universities—and potential employers—also want to know how your kid thinks and approaches problems and whether he can collaborate with people and take another person's perspective. They know that those skills are going to be really important in The Real World.

Question: My husband worries about our daughter more than I do. He thinks she's staying out too late and that we need firmer boundaries. I think she's OK. How do we resolve the difference in our anxiety levels?

Answer: First, your question doesn't necessarily suggest that you have different anxiety levels, though it does sound like you have different expectations on curfew. You'll have to resolve that between yourselves before you can decide whether there's an unsolved problem you need to take up with your daughter. But let's say you and your husband do have different levels of anxiety. If a high level of anxiety causes the anxious parent to overreact, it's common for the less anxious parent to feel the need to tip the scales in one direction or the other, either by joining forces with the co-parent by double-teaming the kid with Plan A (no doubt a well-intentioned show of support for the co-parent but dismissive of the kid's concerns) or by being dismissive of the co-parent's concerns (which understandably causes the co-parent to feel both undermined and even more anxious). Scale tipper isn't usually an especially productive role, however. Being a problem-solving facilitator will be much more productive.

Question: I like to get my friends' advice, and I also read a lot of opinions from experts online or in the news. But sometimes sorting through it all me more uncertain about what I'm doing with my kid. How do I know what's right?

Answer: All those people who are giving you advice probably don't know your kid very well and almost certainly don't have a clue about his concern, perspective, or point of view on a given unsolved problem. So, often the best they can do is provide you with any variety of theories and unilateral, uninformed solutions. The person you should be listening to, first and foremost, is your kid.

Question: What about love? Isn't that what my kid needs most from me?

Answer: Love is wonderful but it's insufficient. Not to mention the fact that, as you've read, there are things parents do to kids in the name of "love"—hitting, for example—that aren't very loving at all. You're showing your kid love not only when you hug him, tuck him in at night, spend time with him, play with him, and buy him that video game he's been wanting, but also when you take the time to listen to him, learn about him, and collaborate with him to help him solve the problems that affect his life.

Question: And patience? Good, right?

Answer: Patience is also a wonderful thing, and it comes in a few forms. There's being patient with the pace of your child's development and his readiness for new developmental hurdles. There's patience in seeing if your child can overcome incompatibilities independently. And there's patience involved in collaborating with your child on solutions to unsolved problems. Just bear in mind that patience alone doesn't solve those problems.

. . . . .

Denise and Charlotte were in the car together on the way to the grocery store.

"Charlotte, can we try to solve another problem together?"

"Yes, Mommy. I like solving problems with you."

Denise smiled. "Oh, good. Well, I noticed that you and Hank sometimes have difficulty watching TV together, and I was hoping you could tell me about that."

"He's mean," said Charlotte.

"How is he mean?"

"And he's bossy, too. He always comes in when I'm watching the TV and makes me watch his shows. He says my shows are for babies."

"That's what I thought was going on. And you don't like his shows?"

"No. It's all sports and *Shark Tank*."

"So let me make sure I understand. You don't want to watch the shows he's watching, and he doesn't want to watch the shows you're watching. And when you're watching your shows, he comes in and makes you watch his. Do I have that right?"

"Yes. His shows are stupid."

"Is there anything else that makes it hard for you and Hank to watch TV together?"

"Um . . . I don't think so."

"OK . . . well, my concern is that when you and Hank have difficulty watching TV together, it turns into a fight and then you usually get upset and then I have to be the referee, and I don't really like being the referee. So I'm wondering if there's a way for you to watch the shows that you like and Hank could watch the shows that he likes without there being a fight and without me having to be the referee."

In the rearview mirror, Denise could see that Charlotte was giving the matter some thought.

"We could buy another TV," suggested Charlotte. "Then I could have a TV and Hank could have a TV."

"Well, that's one possibility. The thing about that is that I don't think we really have the money to buy another TV, so I don't know if that would work so well."

Charlotte pondered further. "We could have a schedule."

"What kind of schedule?"

"Like at school. There could be times when I watch TV and times when Hank watches TV. Nick is always playing video games, so he doesn't really care about watching TV."

"That's an interesting idea. Are there certain times that you especially want to watch TV?"

"Before dinner. That's when my shows are on."

"OK. And I don't really know when Hank's shows are on, so we'd have to ask him about that."

"Hank DVRs his shows," Charlotte observed, "so it doesn't really matter when he watches them."

"I see. Well, I think this could be a very good idea. But I think we need to sit down with Hank to talk about it so we can come up with a solution that works for him too. Do you think you could do that?"

"If he's not mean. Will you be there?"

"Yes—I'll be helping you guys talk about solutions. But I like your schedule idea very much. We'll see what Hank thinks."

The shuttle diplomacy continues. There is now an understanding of the concerns of both parties. The Problem-Solving Facilitator is now ready to bring the kids together to discuss potential solutions.

· · · · ·

Dan was ready for his first formal Plan B with Taylor. A few days earlier, he'd mentioned that he'd like to talk with her about keeping him and Kristin informed of her whereabouts. She'd scowled but didn't reject the idea. They agreed to go out for breakfast on a Sunday morning, one of their occasional traditions.

At breakfast, Taylor seemed to be in a pretty good mood, so Dan was feeling fairly optimistic. "So, you know, I wanted to talk to you a little about us sometimes not knowing where you are," Dan began. "I wanted to hear your thoughts on that."

Taylor looked up from the hot chocolate she'd ordered and wiped away some whipped cream. "Do we really have to do this?"

"Well, we don't have to," Dan said. "But I'm thinking it would be nice to deal with this once and for all. To be perfectly honest, it's not much fun for me to listen to all the arguing that goes on about it between you and Mom. I'm assuming you're tired of the arguing too." (Dan's expression of his concerns was a bit premature, since the Empathy step wasn't yet completed.)

Taylor snorted. "Yeah, but you're assuming that if we talk about it, something will change."

"I don't know if anything will change. But I do want to hear your point of view on it."

"Look, I don't really mind you guys knowing where I am. It's not like I'm doing anything crazy. But I am sixteen years old, so I don't think you guys need to know where I am every second."

Dan was glad Taylor was talking. "OK. You don't mind us knowing where you are, but we don't need to know where you are every second."

"Right," said Taylor. "But the main thing is that I don't want my mother calling me every five minutes to find out where I am and making sure I'm OK. It's embarrassing. And it's really annoying."

Dan wondered if Taylor might become annoyed if he kept mirroring her words, but he did some more reflective listening. "It's embarrassing to have your mother calling you every five minutes to find out where you are and to make sure you're OK."

"Yeah, I mean, it's great that she worries about me, and I'm glad she cares about me, but it's, like, way over the top."

Dan nodded. Taylor kept talking.

"And no matter how much I tell her that, nothing changes."

Dan nodded some more. Taylor talked some more. "So, I don't really know why we're talking about this. I can't change her, you can't change her . . . so it's sort of pointless."

You might be right, Dan thought. He summarized Taylor's concerns. "OK, so let me see if I've got it all. You're glad your mom worries about you; you don't mind us knowing where you are; you don't think we need to know where you are every second; you don't want her calling you every five minutes to find out where you are; no matter how much you try to get her to stop, she keeps doing it; and you don't think there's much either of us can do about it. It's not going to change."

"You got it."

"Is there anything else I need to know about this?"

"Not that I can think of." Taylor looked pleased that the server had brought their breakfast. "Can we, like, not talk about this while we're eating?"

"That's fine," said Dan. "Can we talk about it a little more afterward?"

"I guess."

After they'd finished eating, Dan again summarized what he'd heard. Then he moved forward. "So, I don't think we need to know where you are every second. But we do need to know you're safe. Otherwise, your mother worries herself to death . . . and then she calls your cell phone. And if you don't answer your cell phone, it makes it even worse. So then she just keeps calling. And you're going to be driving the car yourself at some point, so she's going to be even more nervous about that."

Taylor rolled her eyes. "Like I said, I don't mind you guys knowing I'm safe. I mind getting called on my cell phone every five minutes."

Dan gathered his thoughts so he could recap both sets of concerns. "So, I wonder if there's a way for us to know you're safe and to make sure you don't get called on your cell phone every five minutes. See, I think it's kind of a chicken-and-egg thing: your mom calls you to make sure you're safe, you don't answer because it's annoying, then she keeps calling and you keep on not answering."

Taylor didn't seem to disagree with this assessment. "You think she's gonna stop calling me if she knows I'm safe? She doesn't just call me to make sure I'm safe. She calls me with stupid questions that I can answer later. She thinks everything is urgent."

"So you don't want her calling you at all."

"I could handle getting called every so often for something that's really urgent, but she thinks everything is really urgent."

"So her calling you probably isn't going to be the best way for you to let us know you're safe."

"Right."

"So how could you let us know you're safe—and maybe let us know where you are—without a phone call?"

"I could, like, text you guys every so often."

"How would that work?"

"I could text you guys, like, every two hours or so. If she promised not to call me."

177

"Well, whatever we agree to, we're going to have to run it by your mom, to make sure it's going to work for her."

"How come she's not part of this conversation?"

Good question, Dan thought. "I thought it might be better if I talked with you about this first."

"Yeah, but you're not the problem. She is."

"Well, I want to make sure you're safe too. But we do need a solution that'll work for your mom. And as I think about it, I think a text every two hours probably isn't going to be often enough for her, at least in the beginning."

"It's not like I've given you guys a reason not to trust me," said Taylor.

Dan thought about this. "Well, there was that time when you told us you were at the library when you were really at Marco's house."

"That's 'cuz I knew Mom would freak out if she knew I was studying with a guy."

"Right. But that just made her trust you even less. And I don't think trust is the major issue here. We just want to know where you are and that you're safe."

"How 'bout I text every hour? Is that often enough?"

"Well, that would be fine with me. And you can let us know where you are in the text?"

"Yeah."

"What if you forget?"

"Then she can text me. At least if she texts me, I can pretend it's some-one else."

"I think this could work," said Dan. "Let me run it by your mom and see if that solution will work for her."

Taylor nodded her approval.

"Thanks for talking with me about this," said Dan. "I like this better than fighting."

Taylor nodded again. "Maybe Mom can get up her nerve and participate the next time."

"Maybe," said Dan.

What's the take-home message from this dialogue? There are several. First, once again, your kid may be a somewhat reluctant participant in the process. But she does want her concerns to be heard, so it's good that the Empathy step comes first. Second, as you know, kids who have their concerns heard are much more receptive to listening to someone else's concerns. So it's good that the Define-Adult-Concerns step comes second. Third, the kid may have some well-placed skepticism about whether the conversation is actually going to help. That's fine. Fourth, the concerns of both parties are of equal legitimacy. And fifth, so long as you're sticking to concerns—and then potential solutions that address those concerns—you should be in good shape. Everything else is probably extraneous.

Chapter 8

AN ENDURING PARTNERSHIP

In this chapter, we're going to take a look at some of the expectations kids may have difficulty meeting at various points in development and the significant differences between unilateral (Plan A) and collaborative (Plan B) responses to these incompatibilities. And just in case you're wondering when a professional opinion should be sought, we'll cover that too. This isn't an exhaustive overview, just a sampling for illustrative purposes.

INFANCY
· · · · ·

Feeding, sleeping, self-soothing, and development of early social skills are of course among the most crucial expectations placed on infants. A baby communicates much about her evolving skills, preferences, and personality traits in her reaction to and ability to meet these expectations. And parents communicate much to their infant in the manner they respond if she's having difficulty meeting these expectations.

There are many infants who meet these expectations without

great difficulty. And most parents tend to be fairly flexible and are willing to adapt to a baby's preferences on expectations like feeding. However, many parents are far less flexible when it comes to sleeping. Let's say, for example, parents have the expectation that their infant will sleep in a crib in her own room. If the infant is having no difficulty meeting that expectation, then no Plan is needed. But if the infant *is* having difficulty meeting that expectation, then the parents have three familiar options.

If the parents choose to set aside the expectation, at least for now (Plan C), they would perhaps allow the infant to sleep in their bed. But if the parents don't want to set the expectation aside, then they'll have to grapple with the unilateral versus collaborative dichotomy for solving the problem. One possible, and very popular, unilateral solution would be to have the infant cry until she falls asleep in the crib. Hard as it is to listen to one's child sobbing and screaming behind a closed door, most infants eventually get the message—"You're sleeping in a crib in your own room whether you like it or not"—and start sleeping without great protest in the crib in their own room. But it's worth thinking about what other messages you may also be sending:

Our desire for intimacy and sleep trumps whatever concerns you have about sleeping in a crib in your own room.

Our desire for you to be safe—our pediatrician recommended against having you in the bed with us—trumps whatever concerns you have about sleeping in a crib in your own room.

We are not addressing your concerns on this problem.

And Plan B? Because infants can't yet use words to communicate their concerns, parents must try to guess well. As you've read, trying to figure out what's troubling your infant—on this or any other unsolved problem—is where parents demonstrate empathy and responsiveness. Your efforts to be responsive—by applying solutions that address her perceived concerns—are an early form of collaboration. While your infant won't be able to collaborate directly with you on solutions, she will be positively delighted to give you feedback on whether you guessed correctly and whether your intervention is addressing her concerns.

So let's say parents have guessed, or even already observed, that movement—being rocked or being driven in the car—seems to help their baby fall asleep. And let's say that, once asleep, the infant is able to transfer well from the car or from being rocked to the crib. If the solution is to rock the infant or drive her in the car until she falls asleep, and that solution is working well, then your early attempt at Plan B was successful. If not, it's back to the Plan B drawing board. Perhaps the infant is more comfortable and better able to fall asleep if she's close to the parents at night. Another solution, corresponding to this concern, is to place the crib in the parents' bedroom, at least until they decide that they have concerns about that scenario.

What message are you sending when you approach things in this manner?

We hear you. We understand (at least, we're trying to).

We are eager to figure out what's troubling you and eager to try to address your concerns.

We want our concerns to be addressed as well.

These are good messages to be sending. You and your child are going to be on this journey together for a very long time. Good to start partnering and collaborating from the get-go.

Feeding, sleeping, and self-soothing are certainly expectations to take seriously, and if your infant is having difficulty meeting those expectations and your guesses and solutions aren't panning out, there are a variety of professionals—pediatricians, family physicians, lactation specialists, and so forth—who have experience with infants, their potential concerns, and possible solutions (preferably the mutually satisfactory variety) for addressing those concerns. You'll also want to seek out consultation if you have concerns about whether your infant's early socialization skills—responding to social stimuli, facial expressions of emotion, and caregiver attempts to soothe—are developing as expected. Your pediatrician or family physician should ask about these expectations routinely during well-child visits, but you shouldn't wait for well-child visits if you have concerns beforehand.

TODDLERS/PRESCHOOLERS

· · · · ·

Expectations expand dramatically as kids move into the toddler years, especially in the realms of communication and locomotion. There's significant variability across kids in the development of communication and locomotion skills, and it's definitely worth seeking guidance from a pediatrician, family physician, speech and language therapist, or occupational therapist if you have concerns about how your child is progressing. As your child develops the capacity to speak, life can become more challenging in some ways, but this emerging skill can also make it easier to collaborate on solutions. It may be increasingly possible to use Plan B on difficulties that were handled earlier with Plan C.

For example, if a child's parents used Plan C on the expectation of sleeping independently during infancy, they may decide during the toddler years that it's time to raise the bar a little—and improve their own odds of getting more sleep—in which case they'd begin expecting more of *their* concerns about the sleeping arrangements to be addressed as well. It's also during the toddler years that kids begin recognizing distress in others, and this is an early sign of the skill of empathy. The manner in which you respond to distress in your toddler provides an early template to guide her in responding to distress in others.

Among the expectations that cause the greatest angst in parents, and problems in their toddlers, is potty training. As with every other aspect of development, there's significant variability in how individual kids respond to and handle this expectation, and again, we're not going to be especially concerned with how well or poorly someone else's kid is doing in comparison to yours. Many of your fellow parents won't hesitate to tell you the incredible progress their kid is making in a particular realm but may be somewhat less candid about the expectations regarding which their child isn't so stellar.

As with every other aspect of development, your child's response to the potty-training expectation provides you with information about her evolving profile of skills, preferences, and personality traits. Some kids can't wait to get the ball rolling on potty training, perhaps because they've seen an older sibling or a same-aged peer who's meeting the expectation. Some have no interest whatsoever. If you're hell-bent on being done with potty training, you'll miss a lot of information; and if your kid's timeline isn't compatible with yours, you'll also cause a lot of conflict.

But what if, for example, a child won't be admitted into a desired day-care program unless she's potty trained? With Plan C, the parents would be setting aside the expectation, at least for now— perhaps it's an expectation they don't think their child is ready for yet or they're not interested in pushing the envelope on it. If so, perhaps they would enroll their child in a different day care, one that is more flexible on potty training.

But if the parents choose not to set aside the expectation, then they are faced, once again, with the unilateral-versus-collaborative dichotomy on solving the problem. Plan A would have the parents forcing the issue, perhaps by demanding that the child sit on the toilet until she does her thing. *As with most expectations, I've seen far more harm done by pushing the envelope on potty training than by letting a kid's readiness be the primary guide to timing.* Indeed, if their child isn't as enthusiastic about moving things along as her envelope-pushing parents, potty training represents a prime opportunity for power struggles. What messages are we sending when we proceed in this manner?

Our desire for you to attend this preschool trumps whatever concerns you have about commencing potty training.

Our desire to stop dealing with diapers and cleaning you up trumps whatever concerns you have about commencing potty training.

We are not addressing your concerns on this problem.

And Plan B? The Empathy step is, as always, the place to start. If the child is now using words to communicate, then guessing well will be replaced by dialogue. If not, then you're still in the guessing business for now. Here's an example of what the dialogue might sound like:

Parent: Emily, do you want to try sitting on the little potty for a few minutes? Just to see what it's like?

Emily: No!

No? Let's digress here for a moment to talk about your child's use of the word *no*, which tends to be a pretty popular word amongst toddlers. But then, *no* is a pretty popular word for their parents as well. However, there's no reason to let *no* be the impetus for power struggles. It's better to figure out what your child's *no* means, which would not be accomplished by saying, "Not no, yes!" It could mean, "I'm just saying what you often say to me." It could also mean, "I don't feel the same sense of urgency on that expectation as you do." And it could mean, "I'm in the middle of something right now," or, "I haven't really given that expectation much thought yet." And it could just be "reflexive negativity," in which the child is saying no to just about any new idea. It almost certainly doesn't mean, "I don't feel the need to comply with any of your expectations," or, "I'm challenging your authority."

Back to potty training.

Parent: I've noticed that you like watching Mommy when she's sitting on the big potty. How come you don't want to sit on the little potty?

Emily: I don't want to.

Parent: You don't have to. I was just wondering why you don't want to.

Emily: It's scary.

Parent: I see; it's scary. What's scary about it?

Emily: It's scary.

Parent: Yes, I heard you say that. Can you tell me what's scary about it?

Emily: I could fall in.

Parent: Ah, you're worried that you might fall in. That's very good for me to know. Is there anything else that's scary about sitting on the little potty?

Emily: No.

Parent: Are you sure?

Emily: Just that.

Parent: Just the falling-in part?

Emily: And I don't want to get pee-pee or poopy on me.

Parent: Ah, you don't want to get pee-pee or poopy on you. And that could happen if you make a pee-pee or poopy on the little potty?

Emily: Uh-huh.

Parent: This is very good for me to know. Does the pee-pee and poopy get on you when you're wearing a diaper?

Emily: Yes.

Parent: It doesn't bother you when you're wearing a diaper?

Emily: No.

Parent: But it would bother you if you were sitting on the little potty?

Emily: Yes.

Parent: OK. Is there anything else I should know about you not wanting to sit on the little potty?

Emily: No.

Parent: OK. Well, I was just noticing that you've been talking about wanting to wear big-girl underwear, and if you're wearing big-girl underwear, you'd need to make pee-pee and poopy in the potty.

Emily: I don't want to wear big-girl underwear now.

Parent: Ah, OK. Well, you don't have to wear big-girl underwear. I just brought it up because you've been talking about it. But maybe there's a way to make sure you don't fall into the potty and some way to make sure the pee-pee or poopy doesn't get on you so that you could wear big-girl underwear even more.

Emily: You could hold me.

Parent: I could hold on to you while you sit on the little potty?

Emily: And I could sit on the potty and not make pee-pee or poopy.

Parent: Yes, you could do that. I think that's a very good idea. So you would just sit on the potty but not make pee-pee or poopy?

Emily: Yes.

Parent: When should we try it?

Emily: After dinner. Because that's before my bath.

Parent: That sounds like a good time.

Emily: Yes.

Parent: OK. Let's try it then.

Emily: But only a little.

Parent: OK. We'll stop whenever you say you're done.

Are the mom and Emily all the way to getting that expectation met? Not yet. Is that OK? Yes—progress in solving most problems is incremental. Most expectations aren't met in one fell swoop. Do you have to do Plan B formally to accomplish the mission? Not necessarily. But Plan B does tend to structure things so that you don't forget any of the ingredients.

Wait, really? Plan B with a three-year-old?

Yes, really.

Three-year-olds have concerns?

Of course they do. Remember, even infants have concerns.

And three-year-olds can verbalize their concerns?

If they can't, there are a variety of strategies to help you gather information without need of words. Concerns can be depicted in pictures, and Google Images is very helpful in this regard. Just enter a word for a concern and you'll have many pictures to choose from. You can create a laminated card with various concerns depicted in pictures so a child can point at a picture to communicate her concerns. The same approach can be used for creating a "menu" of solutions. While chronological age may seem to be the crucial factor when it comes to participating in Plan B using words, I've worked with three-year-olds who had an easier time participating verbally than some seventeen-year-olds. (You'll find some sample pictures in the Resources section on the website of my nonprofit, Lives in the Balance: www .livesinthebalance.org.)

Some kids are just reluctant to talk. While it's sometimes productive to see if a kid will talk about *that*, there's another strategy that can be useful with reluctant talkers. Teach the kid to rate the accuracy of statements you make using their fingers: five fingers equals "very true," four equals "pretty true," three equals "sort of true," two equals "not very true," and one equals "not true at all." Then start guessing your child's concerns about a particular unsolved problem and see how they rate. Maybe you'll strike gold with one of them. Maybe your child will become frustrated with your lack of insight and start talking!

If Plan B doesn't successfully resolve your child's difficulties with potty training, you'll want to seek out guidance from professionals who have expertise in this realm, though you'll want to be careful of the ones who are fond of Plan A as the recommended approach to solving this problem. The ages at which you should become concerned about difficulties meeting this expectation vary by culture; in some cultures, potty training occurs much earlier in development than it does, for example, in North America. In the United States, many five- and six-year-old children are still wetting the bed at least twice a week, usually because they're having difficulty waking up in response to the body signals that say, "Wake up now . . . before it's too late!" But if your child is still wetting the bed at these ages (and certainly beyond), calling it to the attention of your pediatrician or family physician would make good sense. And if your child is still having difficulty moving her bowels in a toilet at these ages—this is often due, believe it or not, to constipation or other medical problems—that's something to talk to a doctor about as well. You definitely don't want these problems to be a source of conflict between you and your child; conflict won't help you figure out what's making the expectations hard for your child to meet and won't help you and your child solve the problem together.

KINDERGARTENERS

. . . . .

Five-year-olds often have very particular ideas about what they prefer wearing and eating, what they prefer doing for fun, what they feel comfortable doing independently, how they respond to adversity, and how comfortable they are being away from their parents. In other words, by this age kids are providing some very clear signals about their skills, preferences, beliefs, values, personality traits, goals, and direction.

Among the expectations that cause the greatest difficulty at this age is separating from one's parents, typically for purposes of going to school. Once again, there's tremendous variability across kids on this expectation. Some kids venture off and never look back. Often the parents of these kids, while relieved at the ease of separating, also feel the pang that comes with the recognition that the child is fine without them. Other kids are absolutely paralyzed by the prospect of being left with perfect strangers, no matter how enthusiastic adults are about the prospect.

Your child has probably given you some advance warning of how she'll respond to this expectation, because there were probably demands for separating long before the first day of kindergarten, such as for day care or preschool and being left with babysitters or grandparents. Whether or not your child has exhibited hesitation or difficulty separating in the past, there's much to be said for some advance preparation: talking about the first day of kindergarten long before the day comes, and figuring out your child's thoughts on the matter, perhaps by having dolls or other pretend characters role-playing it. Visiting the kindergarten before the first day can be helpful, too, so you and your child can get to know those perfect strangers a little. Still, some kids will surprise you: you're certain that your advance preparation has greased the skids, and they cling to your leg anyway.

Historically, and regrettably, this unsolved problem has often been handled using Plan A: leave the kid with the strangers, and if she freaks out, well, the strangers seem to know what they're doing; and anyway, they won't be strangers forever. While some kids learn to manage when this solution is applied, it's worth pondering whether the mission could have been accomplished another way— and whether the messages to your child are the ones you intended:

Life is full of things we don't want to do; you'll be fine.

My desire not to be late to work trumps whatever misgivings you may have about being left with strangers.

I am not addressing your concerns on this problem.

An alternative response would be Plan C. Maybe the kindergarten teachers will let the parent hang out in the classroom for a few weeks, in which case the demand for separation has been set aside, at least for now, perhaps as a first step toward more incremental progress on the expectation. While this may draw some glances from other parents, hold steady; you know your kid better than they do. It may be embarrassing to have your kid lagging behind a little on the separation expectation, but your knowledge of developmental variability has you well equipped to keep things in perspective. And while you're delighted that the other kids aren't having difficulty separating, you're focused on *your* kid right now. Of course, it won't be possible to do Plan C forever; you do have concerns about the feasibility of hanging out in the kindergarten classroom the entire year. So at some point, you'll probably need to move over to Plan B:

Parent: I've noticed that it's hard for you to stay at kindergarten without me. What's up?

Rachelle: I don't know.

Parent: Well, let's think about it. Because I know it's very hard for you.

Rachelle: Why do I have to go to kindergarten?

Parent: You're getting to be a big girl. And it's good for you to hang out with other kids and learn new things. Plus, there are parts of it that you really like.

Rachelle: I don't want to be a big girl. I want to stay with you.

Parent: I know. I like being with you too. But let's talk about what's hard about staying at kindergarten without me.

Rachelle: I'll miss you.

Parent: Ah, you'll miss me. What do you think about when you think about missing me?

Rachelle: I don't know. I think of your face.

Parent: My face?

Rachelle: Yes.

Parent: So you picture my face? What do you think when you picture my face?

Rachelle: You're my mommy and I want to be with you.

Parent: Anything else?

Rachelle: No.

Parent: Sure?

Rachelle: Um . . .

Parent: Take your time.

Rachelle: It's just a feeling.

Parent: A feeling? What feeling?

Rachelle: I don't know. I don't know how to say it. It's just a feeling.

Parent: A sad feeling? A worried feeling?

Rachelle: Just a feeling.

Parent: I think I know what you mean. Well, here's the thing. I'm not going to be allowed to stay with you at kindergarten forever. Plus, Mommy has lots of things she needs to get done during the day, and I can't do them if I'm at kindergarten with you.

Rachelle: You could do them after kindergarten. I could do them with you.

Parent: Oh, don't worry—there will still be lots of things for us to do together after I pick you up at kindergarten. But I need to do some things while you're at kindergarten. So I'm wondering if there's something we could do about you missing me so I won't be staying at kindergarten the whole time and I can get all the things done that I need to get done. Do you have any ideas?

Rachelle: No.

Parent: Well, let's think about it.

Rachelle: I don't want to stay at kindergarten without you.

Parent: I know. But I wonder if there's some way for you to miss me but not have it bother you so much.

Rachelle: Could you stay in my room for a little while and then sit in the library? Then I could know you're there, even if I can't see you.

Parent: Hmm. That's an interesting idea. So I'd stay with you for a little while and then go sit in the library? And then you'd get used to me not being right there?

Rachelle: Yes.

Parent: Well, we could try that. I think that's a good next step.

Is this problem totally solved? Not yet. Are they on their way? Yes. What would be the next incremental step? That's for the parent and child to discuss. What if the mom can't stay in the library? What if she really has to get to work? Then that solution wouldn't be realistic and mutually satisfactory and they'd need to collaborate on a different solution.

What are you communicating to your child when you approach problems in this way?

I hear you. I understand. I'm reliable. I care about you and your concerns.

I'm not going to leave you in the problem-solving wilderness if you can't meet this expectation on your own.

I'm your partner.

I am eager to figure out what's troubling you and eager to try to address your concerns.

I want my concerns to be addressed as well.

If your child's separation difficulties aren't resolved through use of Plan B, you'll probably want to seek out the guidance of a mental health professional with experience in helping with that expectation. You don't need a diagnosis—just some help from someone who's dealt with it before and may have a broad repertoire of solutions.

ELEMENTARY SCHOOLERS
· · · · ·

The world isn't going to cut your kid any slack during the elementary years. In fact, the social, behavioral, academic, and athletic pressures are going become a lot more intense. And lots of the folks placing demands on your kid are going to be relying on Plan A to "help" your kid when she runs into difficulty.

Of course, these can be very fun years. Kids often really like hanging out with their parents at this age. But, if it hasn't happened already, these are also the years in which your child is likely to be a little less receptive to receiving assistance on solving the problems that affect her life. This is a good sign; it shows that she's moving toward greater independence. Of course, this declining receptivity to assistance could also be a sign that your child has come to expect Plan A from many adults and is becoming increasingly leery of that approach and is beginning to respond in kind.

Let's focus our discussion on academic challenges first. Let's say your child is having difficulty memorizing her multiplication tables. If you set aside the expectation for learning multiplication tables for now—perhaps because your child has other academic difficulties that are of higher priority—then you're using Plan C. Or if she thinks she can handle it on her own and you choose to roll with that for now, that's Plan C too. Just keep watching closely and check in with her periodically to see how she's doing. If she solves the problem on her own, that's outstanding; it'll boost her self-efficacy—her belief in her ability to complete tasks and reach goals—in solving future problems. But if things still aren't going so well, you're going to need a Plan, and once again, you'll have to decide between collaborative and unilateral options.

Your child's teacher probably has some ideas for how to help her memorize her multiplication tables. Let's say the teacher strongly recommends the use of flash cards for solving that problem. If you impose flash cards on your child as the solution, you're using Plan A. And Plan B? You know the routine:

Parent: I've noticed that you've been having difficulty learning your multiplication tables. What's up?

Jordan: Lots of kids aren't good at that yet.

Parent: That's good to know. But I'm more concerned about you.

Jordan: Well, it's not like I'm not trying.

Parent: No, I know you're trying. I've just noticed that you're still having difficulty with it, and I was wondering if you could tell me about it.

Jordan: I'm not that good at memorizing stuff.

Parent: OK. I wasn't too good at that either.

Jordan: You weren't?

Parent: Nope. I used to have to memorize these really long passages when I took Spanish, and then recite them in front of the whole class, and it was really hard for me. So I can understand how it might be hard to memorize the multiplication tables.

Jordan: Did you have trouble memorizing multiplication tables too?

Parent: Not that I recall. But Grandma used to practice them with me in the car, so maybe that's why.

Jordan: Grandma practiced them with you in the car?

Parent: Yep. We'd be driving along and didn't have much to do except listen to Grandma's music, which I didn't like that much, so she'd do the multiplication tables with me.

Jordan: Did you like it?

Parent: Yeah. It made it kinda fun.

Jordan: I hate math.

Parent: Yeah, well, maybe that's because you're having trouble with your multiplication tables.

Jordan: Mr. Jarrett wants me to use flash cards to learn them.

Parent: You don't like that idea?

Jordan: No. It's not helping.

Parent: Well, I think Mr. Jarrett feels it's really important for you to learn them. I do too. It makes the math that's coming up a lot easier.

Jordan: Yeah, that's what he said.

Parent: But that doesn't mean flash cards are the best solution.

Jordan: Right.

Parent: So, I wonder if there's any way for us to help you with memorizing the multiplication tables—besides using the flash cards—so that the math that's coming up won't be hard for you. Do you have any ideas?

Jordan: Could we do what Grandma did?

Parent: You mean practice in the car?

Jordan: Yeah.

Parent: We could do that. Do you think it would help?

Jordan: We could try it. But not when my friends are in the car.

Parent: OK.

If your child's difficulties with academic tasks aren't solved through the use of Plan B, you'll want to talk about it with school staff and may also want to seek the guidance of a mental health professional or neuropsychologist to see if an evaluation might provide some useful information about your child's difficulties and to broaden the consideration of potential solutions. Again, you're looking for more than a diagnosis, though you may *need* a diagnosis if that's something the school requires to provide your child with extra help. What you're looking for is an understanding of your child's profile of skills and a sense of the factors that are interfering with her progress on certain academic tasks. Because some school staff still favor "poor motivation" and "lack of effort" to explain academic difficulties, you'll want to remember some of our key themes—especially *kids do well if they can* and *doing well is preferable*—so that you're well positioned to question motivational explanations for your child's difficulties.

Of course, academics aren't the only thing going on at school. The school classroom also has many behavioral expectations, including sitting still and paying attention for long periods of time, listening to instructions, working and playing well with others, seamlessly moving from one activity to another, and so forth. If your child is having difficulty meeting those expectations, life is going to get interesting. Some educators are much more empathic about individual differences in *learning* than they are about individual differences in *behavior*, even though both realms involve skills. And while you may feel pressured to accept the standard clichés that are frequently applied to children with behavioral challenges—attention seeking, manipulative, unmotivated, limit testing, and so forth—your challenge is to question the conventional wisdom on behavior as well as gently insist that your child's difficulties be viewed through more accurate, compassionate, productive lenses. It's worth pointing out here that 70 to 80 percent of behavior problems at school can be traced back to specific academic tasks a student is having difficulty completing. So it generally doesn't make sense to try to separate behavior from academics; they often go hand in glove.

So it's important to determine the specific conditions in which your child's behavioral challenges at school are occurring—for example, during math or circle time or recess or on the school bus. The behavior will help pinpoint expectations *specific to those contexts* that she's having difficulty meeting. For example, if your child is inattentive, having difficulty getting work done, and talking with her classmates primarily during tasks involving a lot of writing, then the tasks involving the writing would be the unsolved problems, not the behaviors that are the by-product of those problems. If intervention is focused on the behaviors, the problems will never be identified, understood, and solved. Again, the behaviors are *downstream*; the problems causing those behaviors are *upstream*. You want to be focused on what's going on upstream.

As always, Plan A would involve imposing a unilateral solution on those problems—for example, making the child stay in from recess to practice writing. Plan C would involve setting it aside, adapting or modifying it, or seeing if the child can resolve the incompatibility on her own. And Plan B? Here's what the discussion might sound like between a teacher and a student. Yes, this is a book for parents, but there's absolutely no reason to limit Plan B to parent-child problem-solving. It's good to get teachers in on the action as well; after all, they're in one of the helping professions too:

Teacher: I've noticed that you've been having difficulty listening to instructions during science lab. What's up?

Caryn: I don't know.

Teacher: Well, let's think about it a minute. Because I'm noticing that it mostly happens during science lab, not during other activities.

Caryn: You let us talk more during other activities.

Teacher: Tell me more.

Caryn: During other activities, you don't mind us talking to each other or joking around. Then you get all mad at us when we talk during science lab.

Teacher: Ah, I see. I guess it's true; I'm a little more relaxed during other activities.

Caryn: Yeah, so then if people talk or mess around during science lab, you get all mad and put us out in the hall.

Teacher: Yes, I do. So is that mostly it? That's why you're having trouble listening to instructions during science lab? Because I let you talk and joke around more during other activities?

Caryn: Well, I guess it's hard for me to stop talking and joking.

Teacher: I think I understand. Any thoughts on what's hard about that?

Caryn: I don't know. I guess I'm just sociable.

Teacher: Yes, you are very sociable. That's one of the things I like about you.

Caryn: You don't like it during science lab.

Teacher: No, not during science lab. See, my concern is that you guys are working with chemicals during science lab, and the chemicals could hurt people or explode, so I need to run a much tighter ship during science lab. So I guess I can't be so relaxed when the chemicals are out, because I don't want people to get hurt. Does that make sense?

Caryn: Yes.

Teacher: So, I wonder if there's something we could do about the socializing during science lab—especially when we're working with chemicals—so that I can make sure no one gets hurt.

Caryn: It's not like I'm the only one talking and joking around.

Teacher: No, I totally agree with that. I'll be talking with some of your classmates about this too.

Caryn: I didn't know that's why you were stricter during science lab. I don't think it'll be hard for me to be more serious now that I know. And I could help make sure other kids are more serious too.

Teacher: Oh, that would be great. What should I do if I see that you're still having some trouble with this?

Caryn: You could just remind me. But don't send me out of the room.

Teacher: Well, I've been reminding you and it hasn't been working very well. That's why I've been sending you out of the room.

Caryn: Yeah, but now I understand what's going on. I think reminding me will work. But I don't think you're going to need to remind me very often.

Are there really educators who use Plan B? Yes, lots. But regrettably, not enough—not yet anyway. For some, it's because they still have an old-school mentality related to behavior and discipline. But for many, it's because their job performance is now being judged on how well their students perform on high-stakes tests. While standards are a wonderful thing, the obsession with test performance has made many teachers feel like technicians—test-prep robots—rather than people playing a crucial role in preparing a kid for the many different demands and expectations of The Real World. As you've read, among the most prominent of these demands are perspective taking, empathy, problem-solving, and collaboration, and these skills are not taught through high-stakes tests. It's hard for teachers to maintain perspective on the crucial role they play in children's lives, because their current job description is pushing them in a different direction. While you'll want to be empathic toward the teachers, you also want to make sure they're empathic toward your child. Don't forget, by the manner in which we solve problems with kids, we adults are laying down a template for how kids will solve problems with us and others both now and in the future.

If a child's behavior problems are more chronic, they cut across multiple situations, and Plan B hasn't made things better, it makes good sense to consult with a mental health professional to see if he or she can shed some light on things and expand solution repertoires. On some behavior problems, medication will likely be mentioned as an option, especially for hyperactivity, poor impulse control, inattention, irritability, anxiety, obsessions, and explosiveness. Medication can address some of these issues and make it more possible for a child to meet the demands of the environment, but look before you leap. It's important to bear in mind that the behaviors people are concerned about are influenced not only by characteristics of your child but also by characteristics of the environment. There may be environmental modifications that would address the behavior problems before medication is tried. And there may be environmental modifications that are necessary even *after* medication is on board.

It's not that medication should be avoided at all costs; sometimes it's helpful. But you do want to avoid viewing the child as "the problem" and as the one who needs to be "fixed." And especially in the United States, some mental health professionals are a little too quick on the medication trigger.

EARLY ADOLESCENCE
· · · · ·

The demands and expectations placed upon your child in elementary school are significant, but in middle school the academic and social demands increase exponentially. Peer relationships become even more intense, and the peers themselves become capable of both increased compassion and cruelty. Your child is entering puberty— though sometimes faster or slower than same-aged peers—which isn't the traumatic life event it's often made out to be but certainly heightens her awareness of other aspects of life about which she may not have cared much previously. At school, your child now has multiple teachers rather than just the one or two of elementary school, and those teachers often teach hundreds of students in one day rather than just twenty to thirty. Plus, some of those teachers have a "sink or swim" mentality when it comes to middle school and think it's their responsibility to yank your child out of the "womb" of elementary school and into the harsh world of secondary education. (Thankfully, many educators recognize middle school as probably the toughest time of kids' development and play a more compassionate, helpful role.) To all of this, add that your child may become less communicative and less receptive to your efforts to help her navigate life. That kid who used to tell you practically everything is now less forthcoming. That kid who once loved hanging out with you may now be embarrassed to be seen in public with you.

All of these factors can increase tension between parents and kids. And let's add the fact that your child is now much more actively sorting through, making sense out of, and trying hard to get comfortable with her skills, preferences, beliefs, values, personality traits, goals, and direction and sometimes looking a little out of joint in the process (though trying very hard not to). The sorting-through process can result in preferences, beliefs, and values about food choices, clothing, hairstyles, body piercings, and points of view on a variety of issues that may not be compatible with your values, experiences, and wisdom.

To paraphrase Thomas Paine, *these are the times that try parents' souls* . . . and often cause them to shoot for control rather than influence. So we're not done with the collaborative-versus-unilateral dichotomy yet. These are also the times when the helper part of being a partner becomes especially important, particularly as it relates to having thick skin and not taking things personally. If you've already been having Plan B discussions with your child prior to middle school, they are going to serve you well—they've helped you build a foundation for communicating and problem-solving—but they don't guarantee that your child will be supremely enthusiastic about participating in Plan B discussions moving forward. What if you haven't started using Plan B yet? There's no time like the present.

Many kids handle the new demands and expectations of early adolescence without tremendous difficulty, though they all take their lumps. But let's say you've become aware that your child is being mistreated by some of her peers. In the United States, we've poured much time and money into helping kids treat each other kindly and as members of a community (regrettably, those efforts tend to be far more intensive in elementary school than they are afterward), and most states have mandated that schools enact anti-bullying policies. Unfortunately, in many places, these policies have a strong Plan A orientation, which ignores the fact that bullies have often been bullied and are lacking skills themselves—in particular, empathy, perspective taking, and appreciating how one's behavior is affecting others—and often simply drives the bullying underground.

If the anti-bullying curriculum and policies aren't getting the job done, then there's a decent chance your child is still being mistreated by peers. If you decide to watch closely to see if your child can manage things on her own, or if you adopt the mentality that kids have to work these things out amongst themselves, then you'd be using Plan C. If you decide not to set the problem aside, Plan A would have you taking some unilateral action without your child's input or consent— perhaps calling the school principal or guidance counselor to demand that decisive and immediate action be taken against the perpetrator. Given your child's heightened sensitivity to how she's perceived by her peers and increasing aversion to unilateral parental intervention, this may not be the ideal route, as it would communicate to your child that your concerns about the bullying trump her concerns about how you're going about getting your concerns addressed.

And Plan B?

Parent: I've noticed that you haven't been going over to Karla's house to hang out lately. What's up?

Jen: Nothing.

Parent: You sure?

Jen: Um, I don't think she wants to be my friend anymore.

Parent: Hmm. How come?

Jen: I don't know. She kind of turned on me.

Parent: She turned on you. How so?

Jen: But I don't want you, like, calling her mother or anything.

Parent: No, I wouldn't call her mother. Not unless you wanted me to.

Jen: I don't want you to.

Parent: Got it.

Jen: Good.

Parent: So help me understand what you mean that she turned on you.

Jen: Well, she was being kind of mean to Margaret. And Margaret isn't so good at sticking up for herself. So I started hanging out with Margaret more. And I think Karla got mad about that. So she kind of doesn't want to hang out with me anymore.

Parent: That's a tough situation. Though it was very nice of you to support Margaret.

Jen: Yeah, well, now Margaret is the only person who wants to hang out with me. Karla has convinced everyone else to, like, ignore me.

Parent: I'm sorry.

Jen: Like Grandpa always says, no good deed goes unpunished.

Parent: I'm not sure Grandpa is right about that. But I'm very sorry that your good deed hasn't worked out very well, at least so far.

Jen: Whatever.

Parent: Hmm. Are you OK?

Jen: Yes. I mean, Margaret's nice. She's really quiet, but she's actually pretty funny once she opens up. And I still have my friends from soccer.

Parent: But I guess it's kind of hard to have kids who you've been friends with start to ignore you.

Jen: Yes.

Parent: Do you want my help with this?

Jen: No. I mean, I don't know what you could do.

Parent: Well, don't worry. I wouldn't do anything without talking to you about it. But I wonder if there's anything we could do to make things better.

Jen: You know Karla. Once she makes her mind up about someone, it's all over. I mean, I like being her friend, but I don't like when she's mean. So now she's being mean to me.

Parent: Right. Does anyone at school know?

Jen: You mean, like, the teachers?

Parent: Yeah.

Jen: They don't care about this stuff.

Parent: Well, they might. They're supposed to, anyway.

Jen: Don't call my teachers!

Parent: Jen, don't worry—I'm not calling anyone. We're just talking. Like we always have.

Jen: I shouldn't even be talking to you about this.

Parent: No? How come?

Jen: I don't know. I should be able to handle this stuff on my own.

Parent: I see. How come?

Jen: 'Cuz kids my age shouldn't need help from their parents.

Parent: Hmm. I didn't know that. I still talk to Grandma and Grandpa about things that are troubling me.

Jen: You do?

Parent: Sure. Sometimes they have ideas I haven't thought of. And sometimes it's just nice to have someone to talk to about things.

Jen: Well, I don't think anything can be done about this.

Parent: Maybe not. So what are you going to do?

Jen: I guess I'll just see how it goes for a while. Maybe Karla will, like, chill.

Parent: OK. Let me know if things get worse . . . or better. Because I don't think we want to just let this stay this way. Do you know what I mean?

Jen: Yep.

That one started out as Plan B and then turned into Plan C, at least for now, in deference to the kid's wishes. Still, the parent did gather some important information about the problem. If the parent decided not to just let it ride, he or she would return to Plan B to discuss potential courses of action that were realistic and mutually satisfactory. Naturally, the specifics of the situation would determine your sense of urgency on intervention.

Is Plan B "working" even if it takes a while to get the problem solved? Yes, it's working if you know more about your child's concerns than you otherwise would have. It's working if your child listens to and understands your concerns. It's working if you and your child are working together on getting your respective concerns addressed. It's working because you're communicating to your child that you are reliable, that you're curious, that you care, and that you know how to be a good partner.

If Plan B doesn't resolve the difficulties your child is having with academics or peers—and especially if those difficulties become more chronic—you'll want to seek out professional guidance. But you'll be more successful in having your child work with a hired helper if you decide to pursue that course of action collaboratively rather than unilaterally.

ADOLESCENCE

· · · · ·

For some kids, arriving at adolescence means the most tumultuous period of development has passed. Other kids, whose preadolescence may have been relatively uneventful, are just starting to rev the engine. Peer relations and academics are still quite intense during these years, but now the peer culture has added drugs, alcohol, and sex to the mix (though these additions can enter the mix even earlier), along with things like driving, SATs, and college applications. Your desire to have some influence hasn't faded, and the potential for incompatibility still looms large.

By now your kid is presumably quite familiar with your values, wisdom, and experience. The big question is whether both you and your child are clear about your *expectations*. If you don't have clear expectations, your kid (and her peers) will assume you have an "anything goes" mentality, in which case "just about anything" may be what you get. It will be hard to know if your child is meeting your expectations if neither of you knows what they are.

Of course, if you are clear about your expectations, your choices will be the same: watch very closely and see if your kid can work things through on her own (Plan C); modify, or set aside a particular expectation, at least for now (also Plan C); impose unilateral solutions (Plan A); or work together on realistic and mutually satisfactory solutions (Plan B).

So let's get down to the nitty-gritty. What are your expectations when it comes to experimentation with and use of marijuana? Are you OK with her trying it, or is total abstinence your expectation? How flexible are you willing to be if you and your child disagree on the total abstinence part? If you're OK with her trying it, do you have expectations about the conditions under which that will occur? Or are you thinking that smoking marijuana is a relatively harmless rite of passage? After all, you did it (and maybe you still do). By the way, just because many states have decriminalized or legalized marijuana doesn't mean it's a benign substance; it just means the authorities tired of trying to enforce the unenforceable and of spending a fortune trying to do it. Whether or not there's incompatibility between you and your child on the marijuana issue depends completely on where you and she land on these questions. If you don't want her to smoke marijuana, and she has no interest in trying it, you're probably in the clear in the incompatibility department. If there's incompatibility—now you know the mantra—you'll have a problem to solve.

How about alcohol? Are you OK with a few beers at a party? Are you OK with more than that, so long as there's a designated driver? Or is your expectation total abstinence? If so, how flexible are you willing to be if you and your child disagree on setting the bar at total abstinence? What about other substances? Molly? Cocaine? Heroin is increasingly popular these days.

And do you want input on how boyfriends and girlfriends should treat each other? While the hormones (and perhaps her boyfriend and friends) may be telling her to *go, go, go*, you'll need to be clear about whether your expectation is *no, no, no* or *slow, slow, slow*, or whether you're OK having her navigate those waters on her own. Are you OK with casual hookups or do you feel strongly that some meaning should go along with the physical part? Are you OK with practically everything besides intercourse? Are you OK with intercourse so long as there are no sexually transmitted infections or pregnancy? Are you willing to supply birth control? Are you OK with the school providing birth control?

How involved do you want to be in making sure your kid prepares for the SATs? How involved do you want to be in helping your kid with college applications? How involved do you want to be in helping your kid select a college or a different path?

And now let's think about your options for handling incompatibility, though it's not like they've changed. Let's say your daughter and her boyfriend have been pretty serious for a while now and you have an inkling—or maybe you're somehow in the loop on this—that intercourse is now under consideration. You could watch closely to see if she can handle it on her own, perhaps by telling her you trust her instincts and that she's smart enough to know how to avoid getting pregnant and contracting a sexually transmitted infection (Plan C). Plan A would have you forbidding her from engaging in intercourse and, if she refuses to go along with that, forbidding her from dating the guy. You may have an enforcement problem with that one, and there's some chance that approach will end civil communication on the topic as well. And Plan B?

Parent: There's something we should talk about at some point.
Claire: No, please.
Parent: No, please, what?
Claire: It's about Robbie, right?
Parent: Well, actually, yes.
Claire: I don't want to talk about Robbie.

Parent: I didn't think you would. And we don't have to talk about it right now. But there are just a few things I want to talk with you about.

Claire: This is not happening.

Parent: I can tell that you guys are getting pretty serious, and I don't think it would be a crime for us to talk about that a little.

Claire: This is so embarrassing!

Parent: I don't think it has to be embarrassing.

Claire: What are you worried about? Nothing's happened!

Parent: Well, I know that when kids your age have been dating a while, things happen. I want to make sure you're OK.

Claire: I'm OK! Thank you.

Parent: Yes, well, I was hoping for more than that.

Claire: Don't you think this is kind of my business?

Parent: I do think it's kind of your business. But I think it's kind of my business too.

Claire: Fine, but not now! I need to get myself ready for this.

Parent: When?

Claire: Sunday night. No, wait—I'm all stressed about school on Sunday nights. Um . . . Saturday afternoon, after lacrosse practice.

Parent: You sure?

Claire: No—I don't even want to talk to you about this!

Parent: I don't think it'll be as bad as you think.

Claire: I think it'll be worse than I think. How 'bout I promise that if anything, like, really serious is going to happen, we'll use a condom?

Parent: Um, is anything really serious going to happen?

Claire: I'm not sure.

Parent: Do you want something serious to happen?

Claire: I'm not sure.

Parent: Does Robbie want something serious to happen?

Claire: Yes.

Parent: Does Robbie know you're not sure?

Claire: Yes. That's why we haven't done that yet.

Parent: Is Robbie pressuring you?

Claire: Not really.

Parent: So, it looks like we're talking about this now. Should we keep going?

Claire: Oh my God.

Parent: Is it that bad to talk about it?

Claire: No, not really. It's just that it's private. It's . . . my life.

Parent: Yes. I agree that it's your life. But, um, it's always been my role to make sure you're safe and that you're thinking things through, and I'm not quite ready to let that go just yet. It doesn't mean I don't think you're capable of thinking things through on your own. It just means I care about you and want to make sure you're doing things that make sense for you.

Claire: You always told me love makes no sense.

Parent: Yeah, well, getting pregnant would make less sense. And getting a disease would make less sense too.

Claire: They give out free condoms at school.

Parent: Yes, I think I knew that. Do either of you know how to use them?

Claire: I took that human health course at school, like, six years ago! It's not that complicated!

Parent: Is it safe to say that if you don't know if you're ready, then you're not ready?

Claire: I don't know.

Parent: Because, you know, when things get heated, it's harder to say no.

Claire: Oh my God!

Parent: Am I right?

Claire: I can't believe we're talking like this!

Parent: Why shouldn't we be talking like this?

Claire: I don't know.

Parent: Well, it sounds to me like you don't feel like you're being forced into anything.

Claire: It's a little insulting that you think I'd let myself be forced into something . . . and that you think I'd date someone who'd act like that.

Parent: I don't think either of those things. I just wanted to check in with you. And it sounds like you have the contraception part covered.

Claire: Yes, Mom.

Parent: Will you talk to me if you have any concerns about any of this stuff?

Claire: Maybe.

Parent: Do you feel like you're ready for the emotional part of things?

Claire: I'm not doing anything until I feel ready. And like you always say, you don't always know if you're ready until something actually happens. But if it happens—and I'm not saying it's going to—but if it happens and I don't feel good about it, I'll tell you.

Parent: All right.

Claire: We done?

Parent: We're done.

Claire: I think that was harder for you than it was for me.

Parent: I think you may be right.

Those templates for problem-solving and handling distress you laid the foundation for in the earlier years seem to be serving you well here in adolescence. They don't guarantee that things will be seamless, but they'll serve you well.

COLLEGE AND BEYOND
· · · · ·

Think you're done when your kid leaves the nest? Goodness, not by a long shot. By this point, however—if it hasn't happened already—the vast majority of parents are completely convinced that they no longer have control over their kids' lives. Hopefully, your kid now has a better-defined sense of her skills, preferences, beliefs, values, personality traits, goals, and direction, though that journey is always subject to change course depending on life events. But you still have experience, wisdom, and values to offer, and your kid may be even more receptive to what you're bringing to the table. In fact, she may even seek it out. Your kid still needs a partner, just maybe not quite so much and now almost totally on her terms. The ingredients of Plan B don't vary across the ages.

· · · · ·

How you go about dealing with the problems that affect your kid's life—and what you communicate to your child in doing so—colors many things about your relationship with each other, how you communicate, whether you have influence, and whether the problems are actually solved. Pardon the repetition, but you truly do reap what you sow. I've heard many parents say how happy they are that their children are now adults, because their relationship during the child's adolescence—and sometimes even childhood—was horrific, but they can now finally talk to each other. Great that things are better now, but they could have been talking and collaborating all along. Of course, I've known other parents and kids whose relationships with each other never recovered from the conflict and acrimony of those earlier years.

You want to be your child's partner in development, throughout development. While your child may need different things from you across the course of development, she's going to need you to be her partner at every step along the way. And when she starts letting you know that she doesn't need a partner so much anymore, you have solid confirmation that you've been a very good partner.

Q & A

Question: A lot of the examples of Plan B make it sound so easy! Why have my attempts at Plan B been so hard?

Answer: It's definitely not easy. You've read some examples of Plan B going fairly smoothly and other examples where it's been more difficult. There are some topics that are easier to talk about than others. But the biggest difficulties usually arise when a kid is a reluctant participant in the process, quite often because she's become accustomed to Plan A and hasn't noticed that you're approaching things in a less punitive, more collaborative manner. So it may take a while for that to sink in; in the meantime, as you've seen in some examples, her response to Plan B may be off-putting. Hang in there. Even when it feels like your kid is pushing you away, there are often signs that she is increasingly, though grudgingly, participating in the process. That's progress.

But even kids who've had lots of Plan B aren't always enthusiastic about sharing information—that's a common sign of increasing independence—and may communicate the lack of enthusiasm in ways that aren't as civil as parents might prefer. Try hard not to let your kid's tone of voice or attitude get to you. If she's voicing concerns, hearing yours, and offering potential solutions, that's progress, even if she's losing style points. Too many parents get caught up in their kid's manner and fail to notice that their kid is actually participating in the process. It may not be pretty, but it's better than the alternative.

Question: This chapter is making me think back to when my child was very small. I was so clear back then about the kind of relationship I wanted to have with her. It's easy to lose track along the way. Life kind of just takes over. Any thoughts on that?

Answer: It is easy to lose perspective. We're very busy. And many parents become a lot less collaborative as their kids get older and the expectations increase and the stakes feel even higher. It may be useful to think about what you want your child saying about you as a parent when she grows up. You may want to write it down when she's quite young so you can refer back to it later; you're right—things can get a little fuzzy as the years roll on. There are lots of possibilities:

She always got so freaked out about everything that we could never talk about anything.

He was a very good listener.

She was very caring.

He understood.

We never talked. I think he was too busy making a living.

She never really took an interest in my interests.

I don't think he understood me very well.

He worked hard, but he almost never missed one of my games.

She had my back, even when I screwed up.

I felt like I couldn't make any mistakes—he always overreacted.

*I think he stayed in authority-figure role for too long, and I
    needed something else when I got older.*

He had to be right about everything.

She always made me feel like I wasn't good enough.

He always had to have the upper hand.

*She was very wise, and she could tell when I was ready to hear
    her wisdom.*

She loved me, but I was never really sure if she liked me.

He accepted me for who I am.

*She showed she cared by criticizing me—I wish she could have
    shown that she cared in some other way.*

What do you want your child to say about you? That might
be a good thing to start thinking about.

Question: What if, in Plan B, my concerns and my child's
concerns are in direct conflict?

Answer: Concerns can't really be in direct conflict, though
they may reflect completely different perspectives. It's actually when you skip concerns and head straight for solutions
that conflict can arise, not in the form of conflicting concerns
but rather as *conflicting solutions* (a scenario we've already
referred to as a power struggle). Case in point:

Kid: OK if I sleep at Caitlin's tonight?

Parent: Sure, if her mom's home.

*Kid: I think her mom is working the late shift, so she's not
going to be home.*

Parent: Then no.

Kid: Why not?

Parent: Who else is going to be there?

Kid: Theresa and Joni.

Parent: You must be joking. Theresa and Joni are too wild—you know their parents let them drink and do drugs. And from what you've told me, Caitlin gets a little wild when she's with them.

Kid: Yeah, well I don't drink and do drugs.

Parent: I don't want you to be tempted. If the three of them are drinking and doing drugs, I think it's very hard not to get pulled into that.

Kid: They know I don't do that stuff. So they don't try to pull me in.

Parent: This is not up for discussion. I'm not letting you sleep there if Caitlin's mom isn't there.

Kid: You think Caitlin's mom would stop them from drinking or doing drugs? It doesn't really matter if she's not there.

Parent: I'm sorry, but my answer is no.

Kid: Can I go over there for a while and not sleep over?

Parent: No.

Kid: This is such bullshit! Why don't you trust me?!

All right, so that was Plan A. And now, here's the big question: Is Plan A the best long-term strategy on this issue? In other words, is it realistic to believe that depriving the kid of the company of her drug- and alcohol-using friends is going to reliably prevent her from using drugs and alcohol? Is there another way for the parent to get the reassurance she's seeking? Should we try a do-over with Plan B?

Kid: OK if I sleep at Caitlin's tonight?

Parent: Sure, if her mom's home.

Kid: I think her mom is working the late shift, so she's not going to be home.

Parent: I don't love it. Who else is going to be there?

Kid: Theresa and Joni.

Parent: For real? Why do you want to hang with them so badly?

Kid: Well, I really just want to hang with Caitlin. But she invited Theresa and Joni over too. But they're my friends, and I want to hang out with them. I can't just sit home on Saturday nights because some of my friends drink and do drugs.

Parent: I understand. Any boys showing up?

Kid: No boys.

Parent (sighing): I know you don't want to just sit at home on a Saturday night. And I know you have some friends that drink and do drugs. I don't love it that Caitlin's mom isn't going to be there to keep an eye on things.

Kid: Mom, it wouldn't matter if Caitlin's mom is there. She doesn't know what goes on in the basement.

Parent: Great. So I think my concern is that I don't like Theresa and Joni pressuring you to drink and do drugs with them.

Kid: Mom, they know I don't do that stuff. So they don't try to pull me in.

Parent: They don't pressure you at all?

Kid: They offer. I refuse. But they don't, like, ridicule me if I don't participate. They're not like that.

Parent: And you don't feel left out?

Kid: No. It kind of feels good.

Parent: Do you have to sleep over?

Kid: No. I mean, I want to . . . it's more fun. But not if it's going to freak you out.

Parent: Um . . . I think I'd feel better if you didn't sleep over when Caitlin's mom isn't there. But if you really want to, I think I have to trust your judgment.

Kid: We're just going to watch a horror movie and go to sleep. I'm OK.

Parent: You hate horror movies.

Kid: I know. But I'll be OK.

Parent: Will you call me to pick you up if anything's going on that you don't feel OK about?

Kid: Yes.

Parent: I'll have my cell phone next to me.

Kid: I'll call if I need you.

Question: My spouse won't use Plan B—or even read this book. Any advice?

Answer: Do Plan B with your husband or wife. In the Empathy step, you should find out what he or she is thinking. Is he still wearing those old lenses? Is she not feeling confident about her Plan B skills? Does he still think that collaborating is the equivalent of capitulating? Does she fear that, in using Plan B, her concerns won't be heard and addressed?

Many adults use Plan A out of sheer habit. They actually may not have strong beliefs guiding their use of Plan A; it's just the way they were raised, and they've never given the matter much thought. The goal, of course, is to help them give the matter some thought, especially with regard to whether discipline as usual is getting the job done.

One option—as you're about to see with Dan and Kristin—is for the reluctant spouse to sit in on Plan B as an observer. Even just having that parent sit in on Plan B discussions is a good first step. When they see that it's working and see what it looks like they'll be more receptive to trying it themselves.

Question: But my husband says Plan A worked for him when he was a kid. How do I respond to that?

Answer: It depends what he means by "worked." Maybe, after thinking about it a little, he'll come to recognize that it would have been nice for his concerns to have been heard as a child and to have been engaged in solving the problems that affected his life. Maybe he'll even think that would have been good preparation for The Real World.

Question: I've been taught that it's important for parents to be consistent with each other in front of the child so the child can't do any "splitting." So what advice do you give parents if one is using Plan A on an issue and the other disagrees?

Answer: The kid isn't the one doing the splitting in this scenario. If one parent is still using Plan A to solve problems and the other disagrees with that approach, then the parents are *already* split on how to solve problems with their child. If one parent believes that a particular problem is a high priority and the other doesn't, they're already split on that issue as well. So the parents need to huddle up and come to a consensus on which unsolved problems they're working on with the child and which ones they're setting aside for now. Then they need to think about whether Plan A is likely to get the high-priority problems solved. Finally, they need to get better at Plan B, together.

Question: Can you talk a little about how Plan B relates to resilience and self-esteem?

Answer: Resilience and self-esteem are popular buzzwords these days, but we should think about what they really mean. Resilience is the ability to face challenges, work through them step by step, and bounce back stronger than you were before. When the first solution to a problem doesn't get the job done, you foster resilience by revisiting the problem and collaborating on a solution that is more realistic and mutually satisfactory. Self-esteem reflects a person's self-knowledge and sense of mastery in meeting life's various expectations. A lot of parents tell me their child has low self-esteem, that their child doesn't feel very good about herself. But you're helping a child have self-knowledge and achieve a sense of mastery by helping her approach problems in a systematic, organized, proactive, collaborative fashion. The more problems solved, the greater her sense of mastery, not only when it comes to those problems but also when it comes to the ones that haven't even shown up yet.

Question: And self-respect?

Answer: If your child is confident that his concerns are valid; if he has the self-assurance to express those concerns in a way that others can comprehend; if he has the ability to generate solutions that are realistic and mutually satisfactory; if he's feeling comfortable with and living a life that is congruent with his skills, preferences, beliefs, values, personality traits, goals, and direction; and if he's had the benefit of your wisdom, experience, and values; he's probably in pretty good shape in the self-respect department.

Question: It's hard to collaborate if your kid is being dishonest, right?

Answer: Dishonesty is typically a by-product of Plan A, as kids are trying to avoid your wrath or making you mad. But your wrath doesn't promote honesty. As you've read, there's nothing for your child to lie about when you're exploring her concerns and solving problems collaboratively.

Question: Can you say a little more about disrespect?

Answer: Kids' disrespectful demeanor toward adults is also often the by-product of Plan A. When adults learn about and clarify kids' concerns, when they're nonjudgmental about and validate those concerns, children feel respected and reciprocate the respect. So when your child says, "You're the worst parent in the world," there's an unsolved problem (probably being handled with Plan A) that you should instead be solving collaboratively. And when your child says, "I hate you," there's an unsolved problem (probably being handled with Plan A) that you should instead be solving collaboratively. The more you use Plan B, the less your kid will be saying those things.

· · · · ·

After talking with Cheryl at work, Kayla went straight to Brandon's bedroom, as usual. This time he was sitting up in bed, with books in front of him.

"You're awake?"

"I couldn't sleep," Brandon said.

Kayla sat down on the bed next to Brandon. "I'm sorry. What are you reading?"

"History."

"Hmm. I don't think I even know what you're studying in history."

"Right now, World War I."

"Is it interesting?"

"Kind of. But not the way Mrs. Ott teaches it. She just lectures the whole time and we're supposed to write it all down, and I don't understand what she's saying half the time."

"I see," said Kayla. "So you're studying for her class now?"

"Yeah, but it's not going to help, because on her tests she only asks questions that are from what she says in class."

"And you're not able to follow what she's saying in class."

Brandon nodded. "That's why I'm not doing too good on her tests."

Tony appeared at the doorway. "Everything OK in here?"

"Yes, we're fine," Kayla responded.

"How come he's not out of bed yet?"

"We were talking," said Kayla. "We're fine."

Tony held up Brandon's report card. "Yeah, well this isn't fine," said Tony. Kayla suddenly remembered that she'd left the report card on her dresser before she left for work. Brandon looked horrified.

"That's what we're talking about," said Kayla.

Tony came into the bedroom. "If you ask me, we talk too much around here. You wanna let him pull the wool over your eyes, that's your damn business. But I don't let people play me for a fool, especially little kids."

"I don't think he's pulling the wool over anyone's eyes," said Kayla.

"I ask him every night if he needs my help with school, and he always says everything's under control. Failing history is not 'under control.' That C in math is not 'under control.' Geez, how long are you gonna fall for his crap?"

"I'm not falling for anything," said Kayla. "He knows he needs to get better grades."

" 'He knows'? That's it? 'He knows'?" Tony glared at Brandon. "Get your ass out of bed."

Brandon, wide-eyed, didn't move.

"Tony, I don't need your help with this," Kayla implored.

"The hell you don't," said Tony. He reached to grab Brandon's arm to yank him out of the bed. Kayla pushed his arm aside.

"Don't touch him," she snapped. "I said I didn't need your help with this."

Tony tried to pick up Kayla by her arms to move her out of the way. Brandon leapt up and grabbed Tony's arm. Tony swung around and threw Brandon on the floor.

"Leave him be!" Kayla screamed.

Brandon got up off the floor and tried to tackle Tony, who was well more than twice his size. Tony threw him back on the floor. Kayla put her body between Tony and Brandon. "*I said leave him be!*"

Tony stared at Kayla and smirked. "I don't need this," he said. "You wanna let him screw up his life, that's your choice. He's yours."

Tony stalked out of the room. Kayla started to cry. Brandon came over to soothe her. "I'm sorry, Mamma."

Are there any takeaways from this scenario? Only what you already know: humans are at risk for exhibiting their least desirable characteristics when concerns are being ignored and unilateral, uninformed solutions are being applied.

· · · · ·

Denise had arranged a meeting between Charlotte, Hank, and her and they were all now seated at the dining room table. She made sure Hank and Charlotte weren't seated next to each other.

"Can I sit on your lap, Mommy?" Charlotte asked.

"I'd rather you sit in a chair for now," Denise said. "But you can sit on my lap after we're done solving this problem."

Hank began clowning. "I've called you all here for this meeting because . . ." he announced in a feigned officious voice.

Denise interrupted. "Let's get started. I still have to make dinner . . . or maybe I'll just order a pizza."

"I want pizza!" Hank interjected.

"Um . . . maybe . . . but that's actually not what we're talking about right now." Denise took a deep breath and launched Plan B. "I've now spoken with both of you about the TV problem, so I have a good sense of each of your concerns. Now I want to put those concerns back on the table so we can come up with a solution that works for everyone."

Neither child responded unfavorably to this agenda, so Denise continued. "Hank, your concern is that Charlotte is often watching the television so you don't get to watch your shows when you'd like. Charlotte, your concern is that Hank forces you to watch his TV shows. Do I have that right?"

"I think you're doing good, Mommy," said Charlotte.

"Don't forget the part about her being your favorite and you always taking her side," said Hank.

"Well, she's not my favorite, and I know you feel I always take her side, but right now I'm on nobody's side—actually, I think I'm on everybody's side . . . well . . . whatever. I think if we can get this problem solved, you won't feel like I'm always on her side, because we're going to come up with a solution that works for both of you."

There was no additional commentary from Hank or Charlotte, so Denise continued. "I wonder if there's a way," she began, knowing that she had to recap the concerns of both kids, "for us to make sure that Hank can watch some of his shows sometimes without having to make Charlotte watch his shows." She then gave the kids the first crack at coming up with solutions. "Now, both of you told me some ideas that you had about how to solve that, so let's hear those again now that we're all talking about this together."

"You could ask Dad to give you more money so you could buy me a TV," said Hank.

Denise couldn't tell if Hank was serious. "Um, I don't think your dad is going to be giving me more money," she said. "Charlotte, what was your idea?"

"I said we could have a schedule," said Charlotte. "There would be times when I get to watch the TV and times when Hank gets to watch the TV."

Denise looked at Hank. "What do you think of that idea?" She was worried that he'd instantaneously reject any ideas proposed by his younger sister. But he surprised her.

"So, like, you get the TV during certain times and I get the TV during certain times?"

Charlotte nodded. "Mommy, can I sit in your lap now that the problem is solved?"

"What are you, a lapdog?" Hank sneered.

Denise tried to keep things on track. "Hank, quit. Seriously, what do you think of the idea of a TV schedule?"

"Sounds fine to me," said Hank. "All my shows are recorded anyways. It's just that Charlotte thinks she owns the TV, so I don't get to watch unless I take control of the remote."

"I don't think I own the TV," responded Charlotte.

"Well, then how come you're always—"

Denise nipped this detour in the bud. "Hey! I own the TV! Can we get back on track here? Charlotte, when would you want to watch the TV?"

"Right after I get home from Mrs. Travano's," said Charlotte, referring to her day-care provider.

"So that's around six p.m.," Denise clarified. "Hank, you come straight home from school most days, so that gives you time to watch TV before Charlotte even gets here."

"Yeah, but I do homework right when I get home from school," said Hank. "So I don't want to watch TV then. I want to watch TV after."

"So you get home around three thirty. How much time do you spend on homework?"

"At least two hours."

"And you do that right when you get home?"

"No," said Hank. "I relax a little first. But not by watching TV."

"And don't you watch TV when I'm putting Charlotte to bed?"

"Yeah, I guess."

"So, if we're going to go with a schedule, we just need to figure out when both of you would be watching TV."

Hank had a proposal. "How 'bout Charlotte watches for an hour at six p.m. when she gets home from Mrs. Travano's, and I watch from seven on?"

"How long do I get to watch?" asked Charlotte.

"An hour," Hank replied. "That's two episodes of *Modern Family* . . . or one *Phineas and Ferb* and one *Dog with a Blog*."

Charlotte seemed satisfied.

"That work for you, Charlotte?"

Charlotte nodded.

"And Hank, you'd watch after that?" asked Denise.

"Yup."

"And what if I want us to eat dinner as a family, which we sometimes do?" asked Denise. "What does that do to the timing?"

Hank was malleable on this. "She gets an hour, even if dinner gets in the way."

Charlotte thought of something else. "Can I watch what Hank's watching?"

Hank looked surprised. "You mean like *Shark Tank*?"

"Yes. I think Lori is pretty. And she wears pretty clothes."

"You can watch with me," Hank said. "Just don't bug me about changing the channel. And don't ask me to explain what's going on."

"I won't ask you any questions," said Charlotte. "Mommy, can I sit on your lap now?"

"We done?" Denise asked.

"I'm done," said Hank.

"I'm done," said Charlotte, climbing into Denise's lap.

"Do I need to write this down or anything?" Denise asked.

"Nope—we got it," Hank replied.

That wasn't so bad, Denise thought. Then she called the pizzeria.

Your first try at Plan B with two siblings may or may not go this smoothly. Probably not. You may have a lot of old, counterproductive communication habits to weed through. But stick with the basics: one sibling's concerns first, preferably without interruption from the other; the other sibling's concerns next, also uninterrupted; then exploration of solutions that address the concerns of both parties. You're the facilitator, not the referee.

· · · · ·

Dan and Kristin were in the car, driving to the mall.

"I talked to Taylor about the problem of us often not knowing where she is," Dan announced.

"You did?" asked Kristin.

"Yeah, a few days ago."

"And?"

"And I think we came to a possible solution. But I want to make sure it works for you."

"What's the solution?"

"She's going to text us every hour to let us know she's OK and where she is. And if she doesn't text us, we can text her."

"How is that different than me calling her? Geez, that kid is never satisfied."

"Well, I do think there's a difference," said Dan. "When you call her, her friends know it's you. It's embarrassing. When she gets a text, it could be anyone. So it's more anonymous."

"Like it's so embarrassing to have your mother making sure you're safe!" Kristin huffed.

"I think at this age it's embarrassing to have your mother calling to make sure you're safe. Especially if your mother is calling you frequently."

"And what if she doesn't text us? And what if she doesn't respond to my texts—what then?"

"Then we talk about it again. But I think that solution actually might work. And what we're doing now sure as heck isn't working."

Kristin bit back a sarcastic comment and took a deep breath. "OK, so that's the solution. I'm glad you and our daughter were able to talk to each other. Too bad I can't do the same thing."

"Well, that's the thing. I haven't agreed to the solution yet. I told her we needed your input. I think we need to get together—the three of us—to seal the deal."

"The three of us? That'll screw it all up. I'm fine with the deal. You just tell her. I don't want to mess it up."

"Um, I don't really want to be the only one solving problems with Taylor," said Dan.

"Why? You're good at it! I can't even talk to her."

"Well, I would like us to try to do something about that."

"So, what—we're going to all sit down for a little family powwow? Are we gonna sing 'Kumbaya'?"

"Kristin, stop. I know this isn't easy, but let's try it. You don't have to say anything. I can do all the talking."

"That'll be real natural," said Kristin. "I'll just sit there with my hands folded."

"I'm just saying, if it's easier, you don't have to say anything if you don't want to."

"She's willing to do this?"

"Well, it's not like she's wildly enthusiastic about the idea, but she's willing. She is enthusiastic about us getting along better, though she has her doubts about whether it's actually possible." Dan steered the car into a parking space.

"Well, I don't want to be the weak link here," said Kristin.

A few days later, Dan, Kristin, and Taylor sat down for their prearranged meeting in Taylor's bedroom.

Taylor opened the proceedings. "This is *so* weird."

"Yes, it does seem a little strange," said Dan. "We don't sit down and talk like this very often."

"We don't *ever* sit down and talk like this!" said Taylor. "Well, not the three of us, anyway." Taylor looked at Kristin. "Are you gonna say anything?"

"Probably not much," said Kristin. "I think it's better for you and Dad to do the talking."

"Dad and I have already done the talking!" said Taylor.

"Yes," said Dan, "but I wanted your mom to be a party to what we agreed to, so that's why we're doing this right now."

Kristin rolled her eyes. "Fine, let's get this over with."

"So," Dan began, "you and I agreed that you'd text us every hour to let us know where you are and that you're safe. And your mom is good with that solution."

"So this is just the times that I'm not at school or at dance or at volleyball practice, right?" Taylor asked.

"Yes. If we already know where you are, there's no need to text us," said Dan.

"And when am I supposed to do this? Like, at the top of each hour?" asked Taylor.

"Sure, that would work," said Dan, looking to Kristin for her approval. Kristin nodded.

"What if I'm, like, in the middle of dance? I can't text then," Taylor noted.

"No, that would be one of the times that you wouldn't need to text," said Dan.

"And what if I forget?" Taylor asked.

"Then we can text you," said Dan. "Just like we agreed."

"And she'll stop calling me?" Taylor asked.

"If this plan works, she won't have any need to call you," said Dan.

"What if she has some stupid question that can wait until later?" Taylor asked.

"She'll wait until later," said Dan, looking at Kristin again. She nodded again.

"OK, so that's the deal," said Taylor. "Anything else?"

Kristin was unable to hold out any longer. "Are you going to do it?"

"I knew you couldn't stay quiet!" Taylor barked.

"I just want to know if you're actually going to do it," said Kristin.

"Are you going to stop calling me every five minutes?" Taylor demanded.

"Hey! Stop!" said Dan. "I'm operating on the assumption that all of us can do what we're agreeing on. Otherwise, we shouldn't be agreeing to it. If the solution doesn't work, we'll talk about it again."

Taylor and Kristin were silent.

"So let's go with that solution and see how it goes," said Dan.

"Are we done?" asked Taylor, picking up her phone.

"Yes, I think we are," said Dan.

Dan and Kristin left Taylor's bedroom.

"She is so freaking disrespectful," said Kristin when they reached the kitchen.

"I don't know; I thought that went pretty well," said Dan. "Anyway, it was a lot better than you guys screaming at each other."

"Well, she's not going to do it," said Kristin.

"Maybe not. But I actually think she will."

"So we have to do that every time we have a problem to solve with Taylor?" Kristin asked.

"Sure, why not?" said Dan. "And here's the best news. I'm not doing it every time we have a problem to solve with her. I don't want to be the mediator every time. I think you need to try it too."

Is it OK if one parent is better at Plan B than the other, at least in the beginning? It may actually be inevitable. Is it OK to have one parent be the Plan B go-to guy? It's not preferable, but it's better than having no Plan B go-to guy. But the goal is for the parent for whom Plan B is a bit more instinctive to help the other parent get better at it, rather than being dismissive that Plan B doesn't come quite so naturally to the co-parent. The least ideal scenarios are when the parents don't agree on their expectations—so the kid has to navigate the waters of variable expectations—and when one parent is still relying on Plan A while the other is trying to solve problems using Plan B. Parenting is a partnership too. You need to collaborate with each other.

THE BIG PICTURE

We've finally arrived at the much-anticipated chapter 9. You now know more about solving problems collaboratively than you may have thought possible. Now we're ready to consider more explicitly what is perhaps the most important reason to parent in the way described in this book: you want to foster in your child qualities on the more positive side of human nature.

Out of all the qualities on the more positive side of human nature, which ones are the most important? Which ones do we most urgently need to model and try to make sure that our children acquire? Here, as you've read, are among the most crucial:

- Empathy
- Appreciation of how one's actions are affecting others
- Resolving disagreements in ways that do not cause conflict
- Taking another's perspective
- Honesty

When these skills are present, we humans display compassion and cooperation. When these skills are absent, the more noxious side of human nature—insensitivity, conflict, selfishness, depravity, and destruction—rears its head. As we discussed earlier in the book, we are all capable of displaying both ends of the spectrum at various times.

We're told by Yuval Noah Harari (author of *Sapiens: A Brief History of Humankind*) and Steven Pinker (author of *The Better Angels of Our Nature: Why Violence Has Declined*) that the earth is a less violent place now than it's ever been. But it sure doesn't seem that way. The disenfranchised and marginalized among us seem increasingly willing to use extreme acts of violence to have their voices heard and get their concerns addressed, and have increasing access to the weapons to do it. It often seems that our regional, national, and world leaders are increasingly unable to hear one another's concerns, find common ground, and work toward mutually satisfactory solutions. The result is gridlock, polarization, and outright hostility. It turns out that regional, national, and world leaders are prone to the same counterproductive patterns as parents and kids. They're human, too.

So let's return to a question that was posed in the Introduction. Are the ways in which we're disciplining, teaching, and interacting with our kids—and solving the problems that affect their lives— fostering the qualities on the more desirable end of the spectrum? Regrettably, in far too many instances, the answer is no. In our unrelenting enthusiasm for Plan A, we're still modeling the use of power to solve problems and still missing opportunities to help our kids learn how to work toward resolutions that take into account not only their concerns but also the concerns of others.

Another concerning trend: as we are reminded by David Brooks in *The Road to Character*, today's college students score 40 percent lower than their predecessors in their ability to understand what another person is feeling and the median narcissism score has risen 30 percent in two decades. Mr. Brooks argues that the mental space that was once occupied by moral struggle has gradually become occupied by the struggle to achieve. Because communications have become faster and busier, it is harder to pay attention to the voices that come from inside us. Increasing competitive pressure means that we all have to spend more time, energy, and attention on the climb toward success. The meritocratic system pushes us to be big about ourselves, to puff ourselves, to be completely sure of ourselves, and to display and exaggerate our achievements.

We seem to have replaced *father knows best*—in which the concerns of an individual are trumped by the concerns of an authority figure—with *it's all about me*, in which the individual is consumed only with his own concerns. If so, we need a market correction in values. That doesn't mean we need to return to the "good old days," because they weren't that good. It means we need a different model, one that bridges the gap between self-absorption and total selflessness.

So let's think about what that different model will look like. It begins with the recognition that we all want our concerns to be heard, validated, and addressed. And it continues with a technology that permits us to work toward solutions that address those concerns. People—kids, parents, everyone—become angry, frustrated, marginalized, disenfranchised, alienated, and increasingly prone to violence and polarization when those things don't happen.

What we're looking for here is a different kind of power. *The true power of our species is our capacity for characteristics on the more positive side of the spectrum.* Kids need adults to parent, teach, discipline, and interact in ways that foster those characteristics. They can't get there on their own.

And we do have our blind spots: factors that cause us to over-react to problems and behaviors and respond more urgently, power-fully, and unilaterally than is necessary. You've read about parental angst already; here are a few more.

Stress: Life is intense. Raising kids is intense. The race to the "top" is intense, for you *and* your kid. That stress increases the risk for losing perspective, for pushing too hard, for the reactive and unilateral. Badly as you want good things for your kid and yourself, your relationship with your kid is more important. Your value as a parent is not primarily in what you help your kid achieve—what Mr. Brooks refers to as "résumé virtues"—but in the type of person you help him become. While your kid's acceptance into a good college is one objective indicator of a job well done as a parent, his acts of compassion and empathy are too.

Superiority: No question, you have experience and wisdom that your child doesn't possess. But your child has wisdom too—about his skills, preferences, beliefs, values, personality traits, goals, and direction. Used the right way, that combined wisdom can be a won-derful thing. Used the wrong way, it can contribute to *us-versus-them* and *right-versus-wrong* mentalities, and these mentalities can cause us to put more energy into diminishing and dismissing one another than into acknowledging the legitimacy of each other's con-cerns and working toward mutually satisfactory outcomes.

Feeling that your child is taking advantage: Yes, by the mere setup of things, there's imbalance in the exchange of goods and services between you and your child. And yes, he's going to take that for granted sometimes. He's going to disregard your concerns sometimes too. And when you feel that your concerns have been disregarded, you—just like the rest of us—are at risk for responding in very powerful, unilateral ways so as to convincingly and unequivocally turn the tables, sometimes by threatening to withdraw your goods and services. You'll probably be a lot better off reminding your child that you have concerns that need to be addressed as well and that an issue isn't yet settled until that happens. Tit for tat is not an effective approach to solving problems.

Trying too hard: Many successful adults have achieved their goals in life through energy, effort, and persistence. All good qualities. The problem is that, when their child has difficulty meeting certain expectations, those successful adults often respond with energy, effort, and persistence, and assume responsibility for ensuring that the expectations are met. This frequently causes them to blow past the kid's skills, preferences, beliefs, values, personality traits, goals, and direction and miss what's making it hard for the kid to meet a particular expectation. Remember, unsolved problems are shared by you and your kid. Your energy, effort, and persistence alone won't solve them. You still need your partner. That energy, effort, and persistence is still going to come in handy when you're solving problems together.

Feeling that you should have all the answers: After all, you're the adult. The reality is that you can't possibly have all the answers, but that doesn't keep many parents from trying! Parents become very frustrated when the unilateral, uninformed solutions that they're imposing on their kids don't get the job done. No point in gnashing your teeth over unilateral, uninformed solutions; they didn't have good odds from the get-go. Fortunately, you do have a partner (your kid), and if you're willing to hear and address his concerns—and give him the chance to hear and address yours—you're going to have much better odds with the answers you and he come up with together.

Fear of appearing weak: Much of human interaction is viewed through the prism of strength versus weakness. Whether it's sports, business, politics, the legal system, or world affairs, "strength" is admired and "weakness" is scorned. Regrettably, parenting is no exception. But it's a false dichotomy. We humans—parents included—do some very counterproductive things when we're hell-bent on demonstrating how strong we are. Parenting is not a balancing act between strength and weakness. And collaborating with your child on solving the problems that affect his life does not demonstrate weakness. It actually demonstrates strength. And, for all the many different reasons you've been reading about, it's a good strategy too.

Empathy fatigue: We live in the information age, and we are saturated with demands for empathy—people starving and dying from diseases in so many parts of the world, civil wars and atrocities in so many others, refugees dying fleeing their countries, gun violence, tsunamis, floods, maltreatment of animals—and we've habituated to a lot of it. Sadly, that fatigue sometimes causes us to respond with less compassion and empathy in our interactions with our children as well.

Amnesia: While you can still remember some of the mistakes you made during childhood and adolescence, you've forgotten that those mistakes taught you some really important lessons. You've also forgotten that those lessons were better learned through your mistakes than they were by simply having an adult bestow wisdom upon you. And you've forgotten that you weren't so receptive to that wisdom anyway. This might be a good time to start remembering. That doesn't mean you're standing passively by while your kid ruins his life, and it doesn't mean your wisdom will go to waste. It means you need to be smart about how you help your kid benefit from it. It means seeing the forest through the trees.

How does the technology you've been reading about in this book foster the skills on the more positive side of human nature? Let's think about that a little.

QUALITIES FOSTERED
THROUGH USE OF PLAN B

. . . . .

The Empathy step helps your child practice thinking about and clarifying his concerns. It also helps him articulate his concerns in a way that increases the likelihood that those concerns will be taken into account and addressed. What a crucial life skill! So often, we human beings—kids included—exhibit our least desirable traits when we have a concern and can't figure out or articulate what it is. Sometimes that's because we're convinced our concerns won't be heard, as our interaction partner isn't giving us the chance to voice them. Sometimes it's because the emotions associated with the concerns have flooded in too quickly, so we end up expressing powerful emotions rather than the concerns driving those emotions. And sometimes we react in mere anticipation of a battle. The Empathy step slows things down for everyone and helps ensure that we're focused on the right currency: *concerns*, not power.

What do kids learn in the Empathy step? That their concerns are valid and will be heard and addressed rather than being dismissed, disparaged, or belittled. What do parents learn in the Empathy step? How to empathize and take another person's concerns into account. Why are parents so frequently surprised by their child's concerns? As you now know, often because they've never heard them . . . and often because they've never really asked. Kids whose concerns are heard and taken into account are far more receptive to listening to and taking into account the concerns of others. How will you know you're getting there? A conversation like the following will tell you it's so:

Hadley: Mom, I have a problem.

Mother: Do you want to talk about it?

Hadley: Sort of.

Mother: OK, let's talk about it.

Hadley: I think I hurt one of my friends, and I'm not sure what to do about it.

Mother: OK, tell me what happened.

Hadley: Well, you know how I'm friends with Luisa and Marie.

Mother: Yes, I know.

Hadley: And you know they don't get along very well with each other.

Mother: Yes, you've told me that too.

Hadley: And so that kind of puts me in a bad spot sometimes.

Mother: Yes.

Hadley: Well, Marie invited me over to her house last night and didn't invite Luisa. And she told me not to tell Luisa, because she didn't want to have to invite her too.

Mother: OK.

Hadley: So I should have told Marie that I didn't want to lie to Luisa, but I was kind of in a hurry and so I told her I wouldn't tell Luisa.

Mother: OK.

Hadley: And then Luisa called and asked if I could do something with her.

Mother: I think I know where this is heading.

Hadley: Yup. So I lied to Luisa about where I was. And she found out that I was at Marie's. And now she won't talk to me.

Mother: I see.

Hadley: What should I do?

Mother: Well, what are your thoughts on that?

Hadley: Well, I feel really bad that she feels bad. And want to tell her I'm really sorry. But I don't want to throw Marie under the bus. That'll make things even worse.

Mother: OK. Is there a way to apologize to Luisa without throwing Marie under the bus?

Hadley: I think I need to think about it a little more.

Mother: OK. Let me know if you want to talk about it again.

Here's another:

Emily: Dad, can I have the car Saturday morning?

Father: Geez, Em, what do you need it for now?

Emily: Um, I signed up to serve breakfast at the homeless shelter on Saturday mornings.

Father: Say again?

Emily: I'm serving breakfast at the homeless shelter Saturday morning.

Father: When did you decide to do that?

Emily: I don't know . . . I've been thinking about it for a while. I feel bad for those people. Some of my friends say mean things about them . . . like that they're lazy . . . but a lot of 'em are just kind of down on their luck or have psychological problems. I mean, it's pretty obvious.

Father: I don't think it's so obvious to a lot of people. I think it's pretty cool that you want to do it. What time do you have to be there?

Emily: They start serving at seven a.m., so I need to be there at, like, six thirty to set up.

Father: Saturday is the day you sleep late. You sure you want to do this?
Emily: This seems more important.

Your child's ability to communicate about his concerns is vital, since concerns are the currency of Plan B and since durable, mutually satisfactory solutions must address the concerns of both parties. But that ability is important not only for participating in Plan B; it's important in life.

There are many kids in the world—I've worked with them in prisons and residential facilities—who have been on the receiving end of society's most punitive interventions for a very long time. Many of them have given up on being heard and understood. But they still recognize when someone's listening, taking their concerns seriously, and working to ensure that those concerns are addressed. That's when we start to see that they still have the capacity for the better side of human nature.

Our heavy reliance on mental health therapists in Western society may be a clear indication that many people are looking *outside* of their daily relationships in search of being heard and listened to. And what are we talking to our therapists about? Our daily relationships. It's great that there are so many professional listeners, but there's also something sad about the fact that we depend on them so heavily.

Kids learn and practice many skills in the Define-Adult-Concerns step as well, including empathy, taking into account another person's perspective, and appreciating how one's behavior is affecting others. These skills play a huge role in helping us treat each other with compassion and sensitivity. They help us refrain from conduct that is harmful to others. In Western society, we are very reliant on rules and laws and enforcement. But these are *external* controls, and they aren't very reliable when it comes to fostering the better side of human nature. As you've read, the goal is for the controls to be *internal*, and that just doesn't happen without giving kids practice at taking into account the concerns of other people. And yet, the manner in which we often go about solving problems with our kids doesn't teach these skills at all! If you're using Plan A, then you're teaching the exact opposite: you're not being empathic, you're not taking into account your child's perspective, and you're not demonstrating an appreciation of how *your* behavior is affecting *him*.

We humans are vulnerable to being so convinced of the correctness of our position that we justify some of our worst behaviors with the belief that we're *right*. This is where we get very confused between the legitimacy of our *concerns* (which is a given) and the assumed justifiability of the *solutions* we're imposing, and lose track of our empathy and concern for others. If you're imposing solutions, it's guaranteed that someone else's concerns are being swept away. This is not what we want to be teaching our kids! And it's not how we want to go about solving problems with our kids either.

How will you know your kid is moving in the right direction along these lines? Here's a dialogue I had the opportunity to overhear:

Reed (during a pickup basketball game): Foul!

Tucker: That wasn't a foul!

Reed: Dude, you practically knocked me over!

Tucker: Don't be such a wimp! It's a physical game.

Reed: You've been too physical the whole game.

Tucker: So deal with it, wimp.

Reed: I'm dealing with it by calling a foul.

Tucker: Deal with it like a man.

Reed: What does that mean?

Tucker: Right here, right now.

Reed: You mean fight?

Tucker: Yeah, wimp.

Reed: Over a basketball game?

Tucker: Yeah, wimp.

Reed: Dude, I just don't want to get manhandled the whole game. I'm really not interested in fighting with you.

Tucker: Wimp.

Reed: Look, can we play without you fouling me? Otherwise, I don't really want to play.

Tucker: You should go play basketball with the girls.

Reed: OK, I think this is pointless. I think I'm done. Let me know when you can talk about it without fighting.

Parents learn and practice many skills in the Define-Adult-Concerns step as well. As you've read, parents—like kids—frequently aren't clear about their concerns and often merely restate their expectations or impose solutions instead of voicing concerns. Adults learn that their concerns will be both heard and addressed; this is a new experience for many of them, especially outside the context of Plan A.

Many additional skills are practiced in the Invitation, including considering the likely outcomes or consequences of one's actions; considering a range of solutions to a problem; shifting from one's original plan, idea, or solution; and taking into account situational factors that would suggest the need to adjust a plan of action.

How does the Invitation do that? Let's revisit what's going on in this step. You and your child are considering solutions and evaluating the degree to which proposed solutions are realistic and mutually satisfactory. The realistic part gives you and your child invaluable practice at gauging whether both parties are capable of reliably executing their part of a solution. And the mutually satisfactory part gives you and your child practice at ensuring that the concerns of both parties are addressed.

Is it likely that the solution you envisioned *prior* to doing Plan B will be enacted? No, probably not. After all, you hadn't yet done the Empathy step when you envisioned that solution, and therefore the solution wasn't informed by your child's concerns. Is the solution your child envisioned prior to doing Plan B likely to be adopted? Probably not, since the solution he envisioned wasn't informed by your concerns. So you're both getting practice at moving off of your original solution. *In fact, you may also come to find that it really doesn't make much sense to think about solutions until the concerns of both parties are heard and clarified.*

I'm often asked if I ever come across problems that simply cannot be solved in a mutually satisfactory manner. The answer is no. But what I do come across are scenarios in which people have concluded that a problem is unsolvable because their *competing solutions* cannot be reconciled. That's because they've leapt right over concerns and jumped straight into solutions—*uninformed* solutions, which couldn't possibly take into account the concerns of both parties. As you know, there's no such thing as *competing concerns*. One party's concerns aren't more compelling or more important than the other's. Both parties' concerns need to be clarified and addressed. So the only reason a problem would be unsolvable is that there's no way to address the concerns of both parties. That should be a very rare occurrence.

Q & A

Question: Isn't The Real World about power and control, not collaboration?

Answer: There's no doubt that certain aspects of The Real World are about power and control. Certain workplaces are run that way, the legal system tends to work that way, certain countries and political systems work that way too, and there's no denying that your child is going to need to know how to handle things when life swings in that direction. But you probably don't want to use autocracies or systems that were designed to be adversarial as your models for good parenting. The modern world more often requires collaborative processes, not adversarial or dictatorial ones. Fortunately, while there are still power struggles in the world, it's more productive to navigate our way through them skillfully rather than by being adversarial in kind. There's a lot of collaborating going on in the world too, and it's when we're collaborating that the more admirable qualities of human nature shine through.

What if your child has a Plan A boss someday? First, perhaps your child will have the self-awareness to decide he doesn't want to work for a Plan A boss. Or perhaps he'll have the forethought to recognize that his Plan A boss is the means to an end and will have the planning and problem-solving skills to have a good exit strategy. As noted by my friend Tony Wagner—author of books such as *Creating Innovators: The Making of Young People Who Will Change the World* and *The Global Achievement Gap: Why Even Our Best Schools Don't Teach the New Survival Skills Our Children Need*—the odds of your child someday working for a Plan A boss are decreasing. Businesses are increasingly valuing employees (and bosses) who know how to collaborate rather than dictate.

Is the world still going to respond to your child with Plan A sometimes? Yes. If he has trouble meeting the expectation of driving within the speed limit, he could get pulled over by the police and given a citation. Then the judge might impose a fine. And his insurance company might force him to pay a higher premium. If he has difficulty meeting the expectation of getting off his cell phone and fastening his seat belt on an airplane, no one's going to do Plan B with him. Instead, the pilot won't take off until he complies, his fellow passengers may become agitated, and he may ultimately get thrown off the plane. True, some human beings drive within the speed limit in their cars and fasten their seat belts and turn off their cell phones on airplanes because they're fearful of being caught and punished. But others meet those expectations because they recognize that it's safer—for themselves and others—and are cognizant of how their behavior will affect other people. The latter is more reliable. Your child's reasons for doing the right thing hinge a great deal on how you parent and how you go about helping him when he's having difficulty meeting expectations.

If we were to ponder which skill set is more important for life in The Real World—the blind adherence to authority that is trained with Plan A or identifying and articulating one's concerns, taking others' concerns into account, and working toward solutions that are realistic and mutually satisfactory that is trained with Plan B—the answer is fairly obvious. We just need to make sure your parenting reflects that reality.

Question: Aren't most schools very oriented toward Plan A in dealing with students?

Answer: Yes. There's still a lot of Plan A going on in schools when kids don't meet expectations. That's a shame. We lose a lot of kids because discipline in many schools is still so punitive and based primarily on adult-imposed consequences. In the United States, we expel over 100,000 kids from school every year. We dole out over three million suspensions a year and many millions of detentions. And you already know the statistics on corporal punishment in American public schools. Those astronomical figures prove a few things. First, Plan A is still extremely popular in many places. Second, Plan A isn't working; the fact that those numbers are astronomical is the proof. That's because detentions, suspensions, expulsions, and paddlings don't solve any problems. In fact, those interventions are primarily effective at pushing kids away. Obsolete discipline strategies are detrimental not only for behaviorally challenging students; they're counterproductive for everyone in the building.

Fortunately, you may have noticed that some states and schools that are trying to do things differently—trying to reduce the rates of suspension and detention, eliminate the use of corporal punishment, and reduce their reliance on padded rooms—are starting to make the news. Also making the news, and being cast in a negative light, are schools that are still relying on punitive, adversarial interventions. That's progress.

So how does this relate to your parenting? Well, there's a pretty decent chance that, at some point along the way, you're going to receive a call or note from someone at school—a classroom teacher, the school counselor, the principal—letting you know that your child is having difficulty meeting certain academic or behavioral expectations. When that happens, it's possible you'll also feel The Tug: the pressure to extract a pound of flesh, to demonstrate that you're a hard-nosed parent who doesn't shy away from lowering the boom.

Resist The Tug. While you could try to prove to the folks at school that you're good at being tough on your kid, you could surprise everybody and start gathering information from your kid about what's getting in his way and engage the school in a collaborative effort to solve the problem. Educators, who are extremely busy and have more initiatives thrown at them than probably any other profession, are as prone to wanting to fix things *right now!* as everyone else. Help them slow it down for your kid. *Trying to fix things quickly takes a very long time.* That's because quick fixes don't usually work.

The process of solving problems collaboratively with the people at school often starts with a meeting in which you make it clear that coming to an understanding of what's getting in your child's way is the first step. Make sure the school knows you're not trying to make *excuses* for your kid— you're trying to *understand* why he's having difficulty and that the accommodations, adaptations, motivational strategies, and encouragement that they may have applied so far have missed the mark because they were missing the information they needed. Make sure they know you think they have valid, important concerns and that you take those concerns seriously and want to make sure they're addressed. Make sure your kid is involved in the process of solving the problem.

Could schools be a lot more collaborative than they are in dealing with students who are having difficulty meeting academic and behavioral expectations? Absolutely. That's why I wrote my books, *Lost at School* and *Lost and Found*.

Question: Aren't a lot of the skills you're talking about in this chapter taught through religion? And is the fact that we're seeing people treating each other with less empathy partially due to decreased interest and participation in religion in the Western world?

Answer: Yes, it's certainly the case that most religions— when they're interpreted as intended—place an emphasis on treating people with compassion, love, and forgiveness. In some instances, it was the "fear of God" that promoted such behavior, and that would only be an effective mindset if a person believed in and feared God (and even then, people do slip us). But I think many people came to feel that their religion made them go through too many hoops to get to what they were really looking for: inspiration and direct guidance on human relationships, help with solving the problems that arise between us, and fostering the skills on the better side of human nature. It's not enough to talk about those skills once a week; they have to be embedded into the fabric of everyday life. Religion can help people stay in that mindset, but the mindset can also be achieved without religion. Of course, we've also seen religions interpreted in ways that bring out the worst in human beings, and that's extremely unfortunate.

Question: Aren't most of the messages kids are being bombarded with these days more about self-absorption than self-lessness?

Answer: It depends on where you look. While examples of collaboration, empathy, and magnanimity do make the news, the preponderance of messages—especially in advertising—are oriented toward self-absorption, getting one's own needs met (*right now!*), and coming out on top in what we've been told (or sold) is the win-lose proposition called life.

We don't need more winners or losers; we need more people who are oriented toward mutually satisfactory outcomes. We don't need more "I'm right, and you're wrong"; we need more people who know how to listen to each other and validate each other's points of view. Black-and-white thinking may make for good headlines, but gray is the color of meeting minds. We have problems that need to be solved, and we're going to need to tap into our humanity—our more admirable human instincts—to get it done. Those instincts are there, but they need to be fostered.

Question: I just want my child to live a happy, meaningful life. And I want to be happy with my kid. Those are OK goals, yes?
Answer: You'll probably need to give some thought to what you mean by happy and meaningful. Let's turn to Mr. Harari once more, who referenced Nietzsche for the following thought: *If you have a why to live, you can bear almost any how. A meaningful life can be extremely satisfying even in the midst of hardship, whereas a meaningless life is a terrible ordeal no matter how comfortable it is.* And, just in case you were wondering, the most important childhood predictors of life satisfaction in adulthood are emotional health and prosocial behavior. The least important predictor is academic success. Being happy

with your kid is going to depend a lot on the overlap between what you were expecting in your child and what you got. If you have rigid, predetermined notions about who your kid should be, you have a good chance of being unhappy with the hand you've been dealt. If you don't have rigid notions—if you're OK with defining your role as being responsive to the hand you've been dealt and maintaining a balance between having influence and figuring out who your child is, getting comfortable with it, and then helping him live a life that is congruent with it—then you'll probably be just fine.

Question: I've just noticed that the first letters of the five skills you've prioritized spell EARTH. Was that on purpose?

Answer: Well, it's great that it worked out that way. By the way, arranged in a different order, they spell HEART. But I think it's important that Empathy comes first.

· · · · ·

Kayla was waiting for Brandon when he arrived home from school. "We need to talk," she said.

"I know."

"I don't think our current homework arrangement is working out too well," said Kayla.

Brandon agreed.

"So we need to figure out what we're going to do."

Brandon nodded. "I'm sorry I caused a fight between you and Tony."

"I don't think you caused the fight. I think there are some problems that I've been letting slide for a long time, and they just finally came to a head."

"I'm not going to let him lay hands on you," said Brandon.

"I appreciate you standing up for me. But that's my job. And Tony has never done that before. He's promised me it'll never happen again. He felt very bad about it. So I want you to let me worry about that part. But you and me—and maybe Tony—need to solve the homework problem."

Brandon nodded.

"So let's talk about it. Help me understand what's difficult about having Tony help you with your homework."

"He doesn't really help me. He just yells at me and tells me I'm not trying hard enough. But there's a lot of stuff I don't understand. Him yelling at me doesn't help me understand anything. It just makes it worse."

Kayla nodded. "Are there certain homework assignments you especially need help with?"

"History," Brandon said definitively.

"OK, I knew that. What else?"

"Math."

"I knew that one too. What are you doing in math right now?"

"Quadratic equations," said Brandon.

Kayla laughed. "Yeah, well, that's over my head."

Brandon didn't quite appreciate the humor of the situation. "Tony says it's over his head too."

"Anything else?" asked Kayla.

"No—mostly those two things."

"And what do you need help with in history?"

"Everything. I need help studying for the tests, I need help organizing the projects," said Brandon. "I have a project due, like, every two weeks."

"And Tony can't help you with those things?"

"He doesn't try to help me. He just gets mad and tells me I'm lazy. I'm not lazy."

Kayla grimaced. "All right. Well, I don't think of you as lazy either. My

255

concern is that if you don't get the help you need in math and history, your grades in those classes aren't going to be very good. And if we keep having Tony help you, you two are going to keep fighting with each other and you're not going to get the help you need." Kayla paused. Brandon was still listening. "So, I wonder if there's a way for us to get you the help you need in math and history so you and Tony don't keep fighting with each other and your grades in those classes improve."

Brandon pondered this. "There's a math club after school," he said. "But I don't go to it because I have baseball after school."

"You have baseball practice, what, two days a week? And a game one day a week?"

"Uh-huh."

"And the math club—how often does it meet?"

"I don't know."

"Is that something we could find out? I mean, could you do math club on the two days a week that you don't have baseball?"

Brandon agreed to check out this possibility. "But that still leaves history."

"Yes, it does. What can we do about that?"

"You could help me."

"Me? But I have to work, honey."

"What about the days you don't work? That's two days a week . . . sometimes three. You could help me on those days. At night. After baseball . . . and after math club."

Kayla considered this. "I think that could work. Is that enough help?"

"I think so." Brandon seemed pleased with this solution. "Who's going to tell Tony that he's not my homework helper anymore?"

"I'll tell him when he gets home from work," said Kayla. "But I want all of us to talk about it together."

At dinner that night, Kayla began the discussion. "I'm going to be helping Brandon with his homework from now on," she announced.

Tony looked up from his pasta. "When are you going to do that?"

"The days I'm not at work. At night."

Tony chuckled and shook his head. "Mom to the rescue again."

"No, not 'Mom to the rescue,'" said Kayla. "I just think we could use a different solution on the homework."

"Hey, great," said Tony. "You want him, you got him. I'm happy for you to get a taste of his nonsense."

"Well, I guess we'll see how it goes," said Kayla, hoping the conversation would end there.

Tony wasn't done. "He's not always going to have Mom to save the day for him."

"I wasn't thinking I was saving the day for him," said Kayla. "Just looking for ways to help with his homework."

"You gonna save him when he has a boss like me?" Tony asked.

Suddenly, Brandon spoke for himself. "I wouldn't have a boss like you."

Tony was silent as he digested this statement. He chewed his food slowly, staring at Brandon. Then he smiled slightly. Kayla and Brandon glanced at each other, unsure of what to think. Tony's smile broadened further and he nodded his head. "No, I suppose you wouldn't," he chuckled.

Kayla and Brandon looked at Tony, waiting for him to say more.

"Brandon, I gotta say, you don't take nothin' off nobody," Tony laughed. "I guess I gotta respect you for that. If I'd said that to my old man, he would have knocked me to the other side of the room. Now that I think of it, I didn't respect my father much for making me keep my mouth shut."

Kayla exhaled. Brandon looked like he was in shock.

"Dude, I'll tell you what," said Tony. "I'm not giving up on helping you with your homework. If that's OK with you, I'm going to watch your mom help you. And I'm going to keep my mouth shut. We'll see if she does any better than I do. If she does, then I'm going to try it again, but I'm going to do it like she does. I don't want to be your enemy. And I want to make sure what happened yesterday never happens again."

. . . . .

A few months after her Plan B with Hank and Charlotte, Denise had awakened earlier than usual on a school day. She found herself ready for work ten minutes before she had to awaken the kids, and took advantage of the extra time to sit quietly in the kitchen with a cup of coffee. After two minutes enjoying the luxury of thinking about nothing in particular, her mental checklist made its way into her consciousness.

The unsolved problem of Hank skipping breakfast had been solved. She learned that he was having stomachaches after eating cereal in the morning, and they then discovered that lactose intolerance was the culprit. After experimenting with several milk substitutes, Hank was now eating his cereal with almond milk. *Problem solved*, thought Denise.

The solution to the unsolved problem of Hank and Charlotte having difficulty sharing the TV had required some slight scheduling adjustments, but that, too, was going quite well.

Denise had done a Plan B with Nick on his difficulty finding things to do besides playing video games and watching YouTube on his computer. She'd also discovered that he was looking at websites with violent content. Nick had agreed not to visit those websites anymore and to stick to a sixty-minute limit on web browsing on weekdays and seventy-five minutes on weekends. He also agreed not to erase his browsing history, and they figured out how to disable incognito mode, so that Denise could check the websites he'd been on. Those solutions were going well. But Nick still had difficulty finding things to do—he said he had no friends in the neighborhood—so he was now watching TV shows with Charlotte when he wasn't in front of his computer. *That one needs more work*, Denise thought. *Bedtime, tonight.*

What's next? Denise pondered. Hank's grades in geometry and world history weren't great on his last report card. *Gotta talk with him about that this week*, Denise thought. *Just need to talk to him about when.* Hank still wasn't wildly enthusiastic about solving problems collaboratively, but he grudgingly participated.

Charlotte had told her that she didn't want to go to her friend Andrea's birthday party this weekend. Denise had resisted the temptation to tell Charlotte that going to the birthday party wasn't optional. *Gotta find out about that*, Denise thought. *Tonight, when I put her to bed.*

Her thoughts turned again to Nick. *He's not emptying the dishwasher without being told*. Denise decided that was a low priority. *For now, just stick with the problem of finding things to do besides sitting in front of a screen*, she thought. *That kid needs a friend.* She chuckled. *You just decided the solution for him*, she thought. *Still haven't broken that habit.* Then she thought of something else. *He's been very mopey when he comes home from his dad's house lately. Now that's a high priority. That's bedtime, tonight.*

She looked at the clock and inhaled deeply. *Let's get this party started*, she thought.

· · · · ·

About a month after the texting discussion—the solution was working well—Kristin and Taylor were in the house one afternoon after school. Over the past weeks, Kristin had been an official observer while Dan solved several additional problems with Taylor—one about curfew, another about a party she wanted to go to at the home of a classmate whose parents Dan and Kristin didn't know. As Kristin passed by the closed door of Taylor's bedroom, she was startled by what sounded like crying. She stopped and listened. Taylor was definitely crying.

Kristin's immediate reaction was panic. She wished Dan were home. But Dan was out of town. *What to do?* thought Kristin. *She's not going to tell me what's going on.*

Kristin stood by the door, paralyzed. *If she comes out and I'm standing here, she's gonna go nuts*, Kristin thought. *I can't just stand here.*

She started to walk away. Then she stopped, turned around, and knocked gently on the door.

The crying stopped. "What?" came the sharp response.

"You OK?" Kristin asked.

"Yep," Taylor sniffled.

"You don't sound OK."

"What, are you eavesdropping outside my door?!"

"Nope. Just passing by."

"I'm fine."

"Can I come in?"

"Whatever," said Taylor.

Kristin opened the door slowly. Taylor wiped her eyes with her sleeve.

"What's the matter, honey?" Kristin asked.

"It's nothing," said Taylor.

"Didn't sound like nothing."

"Yeah, well it might not be nothing, but I don't want you to get all freaked out," said Taylor.

"Do you want to talk to Dad about it?" Kristin asked. "You could call him."

"Maybe later," said Taylor.

"And you don't want to tell me?"

"No. I don't like telling you stuff. You get all wigged-out over stuff. You think everything's a disaster."

"I do, don't I?" said Kristin.

Taylor was surprised by this acknowledgment. "Yeah, you do."

"And that keeps you from telling me stuff."

"Telling you stuff makes it worse. Plus, I can handle my problems on my own."

"I'm sorry telling me stuff makes things worse. I'm trying really hard not to, you know, overreact like I do. Don't you think I've done a pretty good job of just listening when you're talking to Dad?"

"I guess," said Taylor, still sniffling.

"I know you don't think I can do it, but I could just listen now."

"You're right—I don't think you can do it," Taylor scoffed.

Kristin sat down on Taylor's bed. "I want to try."

Taylor wasn't buying it. "What is this, some kind of psychology experiment?"

"No, just a mother who misses her daughter."

"What does that mean, you miss me?"

"I mean, you and I used to be pretty close a long time ago. And then I got a little carried away with worrying about you, and so you stopped talking to me. And I'm sorry about that. I want you to be able to rely on me."

Taylor wasn't sure what to make of this version of Kristin. "Um, OK."

"So I know this is sappy, but I think I can listen now."

Taylor wasn't sold. "Did you read another book?"

"No, I haven't read anything lately." Kristin smiled. "But I've read a lot of books about how to be a parent, and I'm still not very good at it."

No empathy was forthcoming from Taylor. "And so you want me to start talking to you because you think you can listen now?"

"I don't know . . . I guess I'm hoping maybe you'll give me the chance someday."

Kristin sensed that Taylor was longing to check her cell phone for texts, her default for uncomfortable situations. "Um, OK," Taylor said.

Kristin stood back up. "So, uh, whatever it is that was upsetting you, I'm ready to listen if you ever feel like talking about it." She turned to leave the bedroom.

"Mom?"

"Yes?" Kristin said, turning to Taylor.

"You're not a bad mom."

"That's nice of you to say," said Kristin, feeling the tears coming but trying hard to stay composed.

"You just worry about me too much."

"I want everything to be OK for you."

"Yeah, well, the more you worry about everything being OK for me, the harder it is for things to be OK between you and me. I'm OK if everything's not completely OK in my life. You have stuff that goes wrong in your life and you keep going. I can do that too. Remember that song you used to play in your car? What were the words? *You cry, you learn . . . you scream, you learn . . . you lose, you learn . . . you bleed, you learn . . .* remember?"

Kristin nodded. "I guess I need to let you learn. Just make sure you let me know if you ever need me. I think I can listen now." Kristen hastily left the room and closed the door. As she walked down the stairs, she exhaled and thought to herself, *I can do this.*

Chapter 10

RAISING HUMAN BEINGS

In reading this book, you've examined who you are as a parent, the characteristics you're trying to foster in your child, and your role in her life. Parents have so much guidance being thrown at them that it would be understandable if you decided to just turn on the autopilot and glide with your instincts. However, if you think about what's important, what's not, what your priorities are, and what you're really trying to accomplish, you can avoid feeling overwhelmed by outside influences. At this point, you should have begun to have a pretty good idea of what your priorities and expectations are.

We've established that the most crucial task of your child's development is to figure out who she is—her skills, preferences, beliefs, values, personality traits, goals, and direction—get comfortable with it, and then pursue and live a life that is congruent with it. And we've determined that, as a parent, you have a balance to maintain: get comfortable with who your child is and help her live a life in harmony with that, and make sure she benefits from your wisdom, experience, and values. We've also established that traditional methods for disciplining kids — those emphasizing the use of power and control—are unlikely to help you maintain that balance, and that a new role (Problem-Solving Partner) and a different approach (solving problems collaboratively) will take you further.

We viewed the myriad social, academic, and behavioral expectations placed upon your child over the course of her development through the prism of compatibility and incompatibility. When there's compatibility—between expectations and your child's capacity to meet them—life goes well. When there's incompatibility, there are problems to be solved. How you approach solving those problems has a significant influence on whether they are resolved and on the nature of your relationship with your child. While compatibility is a wonderful thing, it's incompatibility—and resolving it—that fuels most growth.

We've established that *kids do well if they can*, and that *doing well is preferable*, and that the key factor involved in doing well is *skills*, not motivation. As you now know, skills are the engine pulling the train; motivation is the caboose.

You've read quite a bit about how to solve problems collaboratively. Those three steps of Plan B simply formalize some of the most important aspects of being a parent: understanding your child's concern, perspective, or point of view; entering your concerns and point of view into consideration; and working together toward realistic and mutually satisfactory solutions. Solving problems collaboratively may be hard—it might be a departure from the way you were raised—but it's really important. And you can do it.

We've described one of the most important characteristics of being a good partner: *helper*. Helpers don't make things worse; they *help*. Helpers have thick skin and try hard not to let their feelings interfere with helping. Parental anxiety can interfere with helping, but we talked about how to help you maintain perspective so that the anxiety that comes along with caring deeply about your child's well-being doesn't bring out your worst. And there are a bunch of additional factors that can cause you to beat a path to Plan A. Good to be aware of them so you can think about whether that's the best direction to take.

In sum, we've learned that there's fertile ground—the Collaborative Territories—in the peninsula that sits between the Dictatorial Kingdom and the Pushover Provinces. It's not easy to get there; the road has many potholes and there are no nonstop flights. It's hard to stay there; the Dictatorial Kingdom constantly beckons on the horizon. But it's worth the effort to continue tilling the soil and planting the seeds of what you're trying to harvest: influence in the life of your child and the relationship and communication that make it possible. The problems that affect kids' lives do not need to cause conflict. They're just problems that need to be solved.

The collaborative approach to parenting that helps you maintain the balance between having influence and helping your child figure out and live a life congruent with who she is also helps foster the finer qualities of human beings: empathy, honesty, collaboration, resilience, independence, appreciation of how one's actions are affecting others, perspective taking, and resolving disagreements in ways that do not cause conflict. You want your child to possess these characteristics, to be the best version of herself she can be, and to be the best friend, spouse, parent, neighbor, and citizen she can be. Your parenting throughout her childhood will give her the qualities and the capacity to meet the demands of these roles. This is what The Real World is going to require. These are characteristics that The Real World needs from more human beings.

It all starts with how we raise our kids. Are we raising our kids in the ways that foster the better side of human nature? Certainly not as often as we could be. But we do know what we need to do differently. The approach you've been reading about in this book will serve you, your child, and the rest of us very well. The answer to Hillel's question—"If not now, when?"—has never been more clear.

We've reached the end of the book. Your kids are waiting for you.

ACKNOWLEDGMENTS

Numerous people provided feedback on earlier drafts of this book. I am especially indebted to my editor at Simon & Schuster, Shannon Welch, and my editor-for-life, Samantha Martin, for their wisdom, guidance, and patience.

This book reflects the wisdom of the many people who have influenced my thinking over the years, starting, of course, with my family. My maternal grandmother, Clara (Neber) Snider, was a liberated woman way before her time, and had very strong views on many topics; but what she felt most strongly about was her family. My maternal grandfather, Herman Snider, taught me about resilience; his life had many ups and downs—he lost money about as readily as he made it, and he survived a fire—but he kept on keeping on. My paternal grandfather, Henry Greene, taught me the value of humor and not taking oneself too seriously. And my paternal grandmother, Lenore (Sigal) Greene, was tough as nails, an excellent judge of character, and called it like it is. They're no longer among the living, but they're all in this book.

ACKNOWLEDGMENTS

My dad, Irving Greene, died twenty-five years ago; we weren't aware that he was the glue holding the family together until he was gone. My mom is a tenderhearted free spirit who taught me how to care about those who are less fortunate and, later in life, how to overcome adversity. My close relationship with my two siblings, Jill Ammerman and Greg Greene—which might not have been predicted during our childhood—is proof that I'm a lucky brother. They're always there when I need them. My wife, Melissa, is another tenderhearted soul whose courage and resilience in dealing with the struggles of life have been an inspiration.

My good fortune extends beyond my family. The model of parenting described in this book—now called Collaborative & Proactive Solutions—is a hybrid of many different influences, including social learning theory, family systems theory, transactional/reciprocal models of development, goodness-of-fit theory, neuropsychology, and developmental psychopathology. I've had some very good teachers over the years expose me to these models and the brilliant thinkers behind them. I'm a psychologist because, as an undergraduate at the University of Florida, Dr. Betsy Altmaier helped me find my way to the field. In graduate school at Virginia Tech, many others kept the ball rolling, including my mentor, Dr. Thomas Ollendick, and one of my clinical supervisors, Dr. George Clum. Tom taught me about transparency, fairness, and devotion, and about how to think critically. George taught me about people. Many other colleagues across the globe have had a powerful impact as well, just too many to mention here. But you know who you are.

I've also learned many things from the thousands of parents, teachers, and kids I've had the good fortune to work with over the years. What a distinct pleasure and honor it has been to work with you. Thank you for your trust.

But my own kids, Talia and Jacob, have been my best teachers. Being their dad has been the greatest thrill of my life. They've kept me laughing and learning for a very long time. Though I'm mentioning them last, they know they're number one.

INDEX

INDEX

RAISING HUMAN BEINGS

Ross W. Greene, PhD

. . . .

INTRODUCTION

In *Raising Human Beings: Creating a Collaborative Partnership with Your Child*, renowned child psychologist Dr. Ross W. Greene helps parents maintain the balance between helping kids figure out who they are—their skills, preferences, beliefs, values, personality traits, goals, and direction—and ensuring that kids benefit from parents' experience, wisdom, and values. His collaborative, non-punitive, nonadversarial approach helps parents reduce conflict, enhance parent-child communication, and forge a partnership with their kids. With extensive real-life scenarios, Q & A's, and step-by-step instructions, Dr. Greene has written an essential and practical guide that arms parents with all the tools they need to raise kids who are confident, self-aware, empathic, and humane.

TOPICS AND QUESTIONS
FOR DISCUSSION

1. In the very beginning of the book, Dr. Greene writes, "These days, the guidance on how to raise kids is so ubiquitous and so incongruous" (page xi). What does he mean? Do you agree? What are some examples to support his statement?

2. Do you agree that the most crucial task of your child's development is discovering who he or she is (skills, preferences, beliefs, values, personality traits, goals, and direction)? If so, why? If not, what then is the most crucial task?

3. Dr. Greene argues that there are no significant differences between the typical child and the behaviorally challenged child. Why does he make this assertion? Was it surprising to you? Do you agree? Why?

Role Confusion

4. What does Dr. Greene mean when he writes about role confusion? Do you think it is as prevalent as Dr. Greene says? How do you see role confusion in your own household?

5. What are the Dictatorial Kingdom and the Pushover Provinces? Do you see your parenting style falling into either category? What are the flaws of each category? How is making these distinctions helpful for parents?

Incompatibility

6. *Incompatibility* is used to describe moments when a child cannot meet the demands and expectations placed upon him. When is incompatibility a good thing? What is the role of the helper when dealing with this concern? How can you recognize when incompatibility may arise?

7. Why does Dr. Greene suggest that tantrums can be a good sign on page 15? In what manner should you respond to incompatibility?

Business as Usual

8. In Chapter 3, Dr. Greene takes parents through a few traditional exhorting and extorting scenarios. Why aren't they effective? How can punishment interfere with helping kids find their inner voice?

Your Options

9. What are the differences between Plans A, B, and C in the problem-solving goal? What is appealing about this framework? How can you incorporate it into your own parenting?

Solving Problems Together

10. What is the Empathy step of Plan B? Why is it so important to hear, clarify, and understand a child's concerns, and how does doing so demonstrate empathy?

Technical Support

11. What are some things you should avoid doing to keep Plan B from going off the rails? Are there any other things you would add to the list? How can you avoid doing them?

Parental Angst

12. What are the signs that your parental anxiety is over the top? What are your most common sources of anxiety? How can you reduce it?

An Enduring Partnership

13. Discuss the different expectations kids struggle with at various age points. Were there any major expectations you didn't see listed? If so, discuss where they might best fit and how you can approach them.

The Big Picture

14. Throughout the book, you met three different families struggling with various problems. Were these families helpful to you in envisioning how to solve problems collaboratively with your child? What did you learn from the different families? In what ways were they similar to your family?

ENHANCE YOUR BOOK CLUB

1. Practice Plan B in your group. Take turns role-playing situations you are currently dealing with at home and apply Plan B to solving these problems.

2. How can you apply Dr. Greene's Collaborative & Proactive Solutions (CPS) method to problems outside the realm of parenting? Discuss ways in which this method can be used with friends, coworkers, and other adults in your life.

ABOUT THE AUTHOR

Ross W. Greene, PhD, is the founder and director of Lives in the Balance (www.livesinthebalance.org) and the originator of the Collaborative & Proactive Solutions approach. He served on the faculty at Harvard Medical School for over twenty years and is now on the adjunct faculty in the psychology department at Virginia Tech and in the Faculty of Science at University of Technology in Sydney, Australia. Dr. Greene consults extensively to general and special education schools, inpatient psychiatric units, and residential and juvenile detention facilities. He lectures extensively throughout the world. His research has been funded by the United States Department of Education, the National Institute on Drug Abuse, the Stanley Medical Research Institute, and the Maine Juvenile Justice Advisory Group. He lives in Maine.